an
Association.

STEMI
PROVIDER MANUAL

Editor

Elizabeth Sinz, MD, *Associate
Science Editor*

Senior Managing Editor

Erik S. Soderberg, MS

Special Contributors

Steven C. Brooks, MD
Clifton W. Callaway, MD, PhD
Louis Gonzales, BS, LP
Sallie Young, PharmD, BCPS,
Pharmacotherapy Editor

ACLS Subcommittee 2011-2012

Clifton W. Callaway, MD, PhD, *Chair*
Robert W. Neumar, MD, PhD, *Immediate
Past Chair, 2008-2010*
Michael Donnino, MD
Andrea Gabrielli, MD
Raúl J. Gazmuri, MD, PhD
Romergryko Geocadin, MD
Erik Hess, MD, MSc
Edward C. Jauch, MD, MS
Richard Kerber, MD
Eric Lavonas, MD
Ronald M. Lazar, PhD
Venu Menon, MD
Laurie J. Morrison, MD, MSc
Graham Nichol, MD, MPH
Brian O'Neil, MD
Joseph P. Ornato, MD
Mary Ann Peberdy, MD
Scott M. Silvers, MD
Mintu Turakhia, MD, MS
Terry L. Vanden Hoek, MD
Demetris Yannopoulos, MD
Janice L. Zimmerman, MD

© 2011 American Heart Association
ISBN 978-1-61669-248-3
Printed in the United States of America

First American Heart Association Printing November 2011
10 9 8 7 6 5 4

ACLS Subcommittee 2010-2011

Clifton W. Callaway, MD, PhD, *Chair*
Robert W. Neumar, MD, PhD, *Immediate
    Past Chair, 2008-2010*
Steven Brooks, MD
Daniel P. Davis, MD
Michael Donnino, MD
Andrea Gabrielli, MD
Romergryko Geocadin, MD
Erik Hess, MD, MSc
Mark S. Link, MD
Bryan McNally, MD, MPH
Venu Menon, MD
Graham Nichol, MD, MPH
Brian O'Neil, MD
Joseph P. Ornato, MD
Charles W. Otto, MD
Michael Shuster, MD
Scott M. Silvers, MD
Mintu Turakhia, MD, MS
Terry L. Vanden Hoek, MD
Janice L. Zimmerman, MD

Acknowledgment

Allen McCullough, PhD

To find out about any updates or corrections to this text, visit **www.heart.org/cpr**, navigate to the page for this text, and click on "Updates."

Contents

Preface

The mission of the American Heart Association is building healthier lives, free of cardiovascular diseases and stroke. This manual aims to prevent death and ST-segment elevation myocardial infarction (STEMI) and reduce disability by promoting early reperfusion of the myocardium involved in STEMI. Emphasized is the importance of a comprehensive and interdisciplinary team approach to the patient with STEMI.

Description

About every 25 seconds someone in America will have a coronary event, and every minute someone dies from one. Coronary heart disease caused 1 of every 6 deaths in the United States in 2007. Each year an estimated 785 000 Americans will have a new coronary attack, and about 470 000 will have a recurrent attack.

An effective, time-dependent treatment for STEMI necessitates the education of healthcare providers as well as the general public about prompt treatment for STEMI. STEMI is an essential part of the Advanced Cardiovascular Life Support (ACLS) course.

ACLS is a dynamic process in which scientific developments are continually evaluated with respect to current recommendations. The ACLS network of providers, instructors, affiliate faculty, and national faculty is one mechanism of providing guidelines and protocols for healthcare providers to institute prompt treatment of STEMI.

Medical care is evolving into a discipline marked by effective teamwork. Patients with serious illnesses such as STEMI need well-coordinated interdisciplinary teams for optimal treatment. The team begins with the patients and their families and coworkers learning CPR, understanding how to access the emergency medical services (EMS) system, and learning the warning signs of STEMI. It

continues with the EMS and hospital emergency care systems through hospitalization to posthospital care.

It is precisely because these events require effective teamwork and are time-dependent that they lend themselves so well to protocols and guidelines. The ACLS scenarios enable us to understand what to do when faced with medical emergencies. ACLS encourages us to develop protocols that fit with our local environment to optimize care for our patients. ACLS helps us act promptly when faced with a medical emergency such as STEMI.

Date of original release: June 2008

Date of revision: September 2011

Date of expiration: October 31, 2014

Target Audience

The medical professions targeted for this learning activity are prehospital and emergency department (ED) healthcare providers (eg, paramedics, nurses, physicians).

Learning Objectives

Upon completion of this independent study you will be able to

1. List the actions prehospital and ED healthcare providers need to initiate to improve the STEMI Systems of Care
2. Identify the 12-lead ECG as a key tool that must be used to triage and treat an acute coronary syndrome (ACS)
3. Recognize the ACS Algorithm as a tool to identify a patient who is experiencing chest discomfort and to guide the initial steps that prehospital and ED healthcare providers must take to manage a STEMI patient
4. Differentiate the ECG findings for categorizing into 1 of 3 possible groups: ST-segment elevation, ST-segment depression, or normal or nondiagnostic ECG

5. Identify steps needed to attain the treatment goals to treat eligible STEMI patients with either fibrinolytic therapy within 30 minutes or with percutaneous coronary intervention (PCI) within 90 minutes of arrival at the ED

6. Identify appropriate pharmacologic agents for discomfort relief and as aids to reperfusion therapy

Instructions for Independent Study

This material is designed for you to study and learn at your own pace. There is no additional fee for continuing education credit for this material.

- Review the learning objectives.
- Read the text.
- Take the online test and evaluation.
- Print the completion and CE certificates.

There are ten annotated 12-lead ECGs provided for self study.

The test, evaluation, and certificate can be accessed at **www.OnlineAHA.org/STEMI**.

If you have never registered on this site, you will need to register before accessing the test, evaluation, and certificate.

Accreditation/Designation Statements

Continuing Medical Education Accreditation — Physicians
The American Heart Association is accredited by the Accreditation Council for Continuing Medical Education to provide continuing medical education for physicians.

The American Heart Association designates this educational activity for a maximum of 1.50 *AMA PRA Category 1 Credits™*. Physicians should only claim credit commensurate with the extent of their participation in the activity.

All faculty participating in CME/CE activities sponsored by The American Heart Association will disclose to the audience (1) significant financial relationships with the manufacturer(s) of products from the commercial supporter(s) and/or the manufacturer(s) of products or devices discussed in their presentation, and (2) unlabeled/unapproved uses of drugs or devices discussed in their presentation. Such disclosures will be made in writing in course presentation materials.

Continuing Medical Education Accreditation — Physician Assistants
AAPA accepts Category 1 credit from AOACCME, Prescribed credit from AAFP, and *AMA PRA Category 1 Credit™* from organizations accredited by ACCME. This activity was designated for 1.50 *AMA PRA Category 1 Credit™*.

Continuing Education Accreditation — Nurses
This program has been approved by the American Association of Critical Care Nurses (AACN) for 1.50 Contact Hours.

Continuing Education Accreditation — Emergency Medical Services
This continuing education activity is approved by the American Heart Association, an organization accredited by the Continuing Education Coordinating Board for Emergency Medical Services (CECBEMS), for 1.50 Advanced CEHs, activity number 11-AMHA-F3-0132.

Disclosure

As a sponsor accredited by the Accreditation Council for Continuing Medical Education (ACCME) and the American Association of Critical Care Nurses (AACN), the American Heart Association must ensure fair balance, independence, objectivity, and scientific rigor in all its individually sponsored or jointly sponsored educational activities. Therefore, all faculty and authors participating in continuing education activities sponsored by the American Heart Association must disclose to the audience: (1) any significant financial relationships with the manufacturer(s) of products from the commercial supporter(s) and/or the manufacturer(s) of products or devices discussed in the activity, and (2) unlabeled/unapproved uses of drugs or devices discussed in the activity. The intent of this disclosure is not to prevent an author with a significant financial or other relationship from contributing, but rather to provide participants with information with which they can make their own judgments. It remains for the participants to determine whether the author's interests or relationships may influence the content.

I. The following editors have declared financial interest(s) and/or affiliations:

Name	Relationship/ Financial Interest	Name of Firm
Steven Brooks, MD	Research grant	Laerdal Foundation for Acute Medicine
Clifton W. Callaway, MD, PhD	Speaker honoraria Stock owner Co-inventor	Apple Computer, Inc. Medtronic ERS

II. The following faculty/editors have declared NO financial interest(s) and/or affiliations:
Louis Gonzales, EMT-P
Elizabeth Sinz, MD
Erik Soderberg, MS
Sallie Young, PharmD, BCPS

III. Institutional Disclosure
The American Heart Association has not received any funding from commercial sources in support of this educational activity.

Unlabeled Uses of Products
The continuing education booklet *STEMI Provider Manual* contains recommendations from the American Heart Association Emergency Cardiovascular Care Committee, Subcommittee on Advanced Cardiovascular Life Support and the American College of Cardiology. Most of these recommendations are based on guidelines developed in an evidence evaluation consensus process for the International Guidelines 2005 and 2010 Conference. The evidence evaluation consists of expert review, analysis, and discussion of published relevant scientific studies.

The drug treatments recommended in this text are consistent with Food and Drug Administration (FDA) and/or ACC/AHA Guidelines recommendations.

"Healthcare providers acting during the first several hours after symptom onset frequently determine the magnitude of any benefit from treatment and intervention.... Cooperation, coordination, and a highly efficient system of care that speeds the diagnosis and provides the right treatment at the right time for ACS STEMI patients are paramount to reducing mortality and optimizing the benefit from any acute cardiac care strategy."

ACLS and emergency healthcare providers play a pivotal role in the management of patients with possible acute coronary syndromes. Many of these patients need time-dependent therapies that can have an impact on outcome (eg, heart failure and death). Patients with ST-segment elevation myocardial infarction (STEMI) and those STEMI patients with cardiogenic shock or at high risk for developing heart failure require specialized centers for treatment. Cardiologists are ultimately involved in the care of these patients, but healthcare providers acting during the first several hours after symptom onset frequently determine the magnitude of any benefit from treatment and intervention. Similar to trauma systems, cooperation, coordination, and a highly efficient system of care that speeds the diagnosis and provides the right treatment at the right time are paramount to reducing mortality and optimizing the benefit from any acute cardiac care strategy.

This focused provider manual will review the basic concept of an interdisciplinary and co-dependent system for the provision of timely care. Based on an understanding of the pathophysiology of acute coronary syndromes, this book will provide you with the essentials of symptom evaluation, initial triage, and treatment of a patient presenting with chest discomfort. This manual also identifies the 12-lead ECG as a central component for triage of patients with chest discomfort.

Highlights from AHA Conference Proceedings: STEMI Systems of Care
Call to Action

- 30% of STEMI patients receive no reperfusion therapy despite availability and absence of contraindications.

- Less than 50% of patients treated with fibrinolysis have a door-to-needle time within 30 minutes.

- Only 35% of patients treated with PCI have a door-to-balloon time within 90 minutes.

- 20% of STEMI patients have contraindications to fibrinolytic therapy, but 70% of these patients do not receive reperfusion with PCI.

- EMS activation of the cardiac catheterization laboratory speeds the time to diagnosis and reperfusion therapy, but about 75% of patients drive themselves or are transported by family or friends to the hospital.

"Timely reperfusion of the STEMI patient is an interdisciplinary responsibility, a system challenge, and an individual provider's priority."

Rapid reperfusion of the patient with STEMI, optimal adjunctive treatment, interdisciplinary care, and optimal discharge medical therapy improve the outcome of patients with acute coronary syndromes.[1-18] Timely reperfusion of the STEMI patient is an interdisciplinary responsibility, a system challenge, and an individual provider's priority. Similar to the "chain of survival" for cardiac arrest, the STEMI patient also has a chain of survival. There is a short window of time when infarct artery patency can impact myocardial salvage, preserve left ventricular function, and optimize recovery and long term prognosis (Figure 1).

Reducing the time from onset of symptoms to establishment of coronary artery patency in STEMI is critical[1] and embodies the concept "time is muscle." The "links" in the STEMI Chain of Survival can be divided into 4 components: time from symptom onset until patient recognition and decision to seek medical help; EMS activation, evaluation, treatment, and transport; emergency department (ED) evaluation and initiation of a reperfusion strategy; and pharmacologic or mechanical reperfusion therapy.[19]

A system is a group of regularly interacting and interdependent components. The system provides the links for the chain, the material to construct it with, and determines the strength of each link and the chain as a whole. By definition, the system determines the ultimate outcome and strength of the chain and provides collective support and organization. While no chain is stronger than its weakest link, it is also no stronger than the material and method of assembly for the entire piece. For patients with possible acute coronary syndromes the system rapidly triages patients, determines a possible or provisional diagnosis, and initiates a strategy based upon initial clinical characteristics.

STEMI—Goals of Therapy

The primary goals of reperfusion therapy in patients with STEMI are to

- Prevent or minimize myocardial damage (infarct size)
- Prevent major adverse cardiac events and complications—serious or fatal cardiac arrhythmias, congestive heart failure, rupture of the heart, and death
- Anticipate and treat life-threatening complications

Complete occlusion of an epicardial coronary artery eventually produces elevation of the ST segment in the

Figure 1. The STEMI Chain of Survival.[19]

ECG of most patients. Myocardial cell (myocyte) death begins and proceeds rapidly from subendocardium to epicardium in a region supplied by the coronary artery unless flow is reestablished (Figure 2). In a minority of patients the clot resolves spontaneously. In all others, fibrinolytic therapy or mechanical reperfusion with PCI using balloons and stents early after the onset of occlusion is necessary to limit myocardial damage. Loss of heart muscle is time dependent—*time is muscle*. The majority of myocyte necrosis (ie, MI) occurs within the first several hours. Reperfusion has been shown to reduce mortality, preserve LV function, and prevent or attenuate the development of congestive heart failure.

Traditional benchmarks for reperfusion therapy have been a door-to needle time within 30 minutes and a door-to-balloon time within 90 minutes. However, myocardial ischemia starts when the epicardial artery is occluded, clinically identified as the onset of continuous persistent chest discomfort (or ischemic symptom equivalent). It is the "total ischemic time" (time from symptom onset to intervention) that ultimately determines mortality and morbidity. The system goal for total ischemic time should be less than 120 minutes (Figure 3 and Table 1). There are four intervals that comprise total ischemic time: 1) symptom onset–to–EMS arrival; 2) EMS arrival–to–hospital arrival; 3) hospital arrival–to-ECG; 4) ECG-to-drug/balloon. A prehospital ECG impacts the last three time intervals and completely eliminates the need for

the third interval. Reducing total ischemic time has been problematic because patient and physician educational efforts and community awareness programs have not been successful.[20,21] Ideally, a community-wide educational program should address barriers to patient recognition of symptoms and activation of EMS.

Improving Access and Reducing Delays

STEMI systems of care have several components that are vital for functional operation. At the core of the system is the patient (and family, friends, or coworkers) who must act in a timely manner to recognize symptoms; EMS systems and personnel who need to identify the suspected ACS patient rapidly, EMS providers who must perform a 12-lead ECG to identify STEMI and then triage patients to an appropriate facility; and hospitals that maintain and monitor an interdisciplinary system of STEMI care treatment. However, there are many additional "stakeholders" who must be brought into the system. These include physicians, administrative and hospital support personnel, third-party payers, and government and regional EMS committees (Figure 4).

Any delay in coronary reperfusion reduces the effectiveness of fibrinolytic-based or catheter-based therapy, increases mortality, and decreases myocardial salvage. Because the potential for myocardial salvage decreases with time and

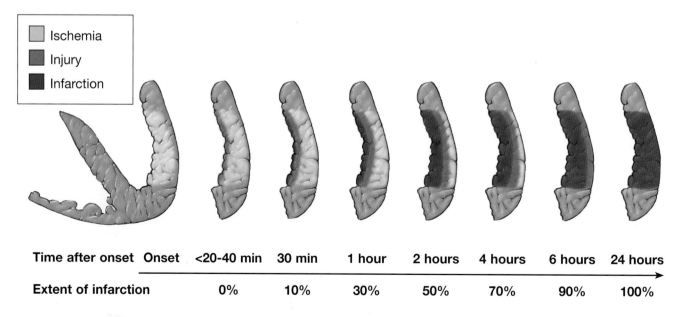

Figure 2. After occlusion of a coronary artery, progressive cell death occurs. Note that the majority of myocardial infarction occurs by 4 hours after the onset of symptoms. After 6 hours the infarct is nearly complete. The extent and degree of myocardial infarction depends on several factors: the coronary artery involved, the amount of myocardium downstream from the occlusion, the degree and duration of occlusion, and the presence or absence of collateral supply.

Table 1. Initial Reperfusion Goals for Patients With STEMI Based Upon (1) EMS System Transport (Preferred and Recommended) or (2) Patient Self-Transport (Discouraged). Modified from 2009 Focused Updates: ACC/AHA/SCAI STEMI/ PCI Guidelines.[22,22A]

Medical System Goals: EMS Transport (Recommended)

- In the US prehospital fibrinolysis is infrequent, but if EMS has fibrinolytic capability, drug administration should be started as soon as possible and within 30 minutes of arrival of EMS on the scene. For the majority of patients with STEMI, advance notification of the receiving hospital and STEMI care team should be made and the patient should be transported rapidly to the receiving facility. The **medical contact-to-needle** time should be within 30 minutes. Medical contact occurs when paramedics first arrive at the scene.
- If primary PCI has been determined to be the reperfusion modality of choice, the **EMS arrival-to-balloon** time should be as soon as possible and within 90 minutes.
- If EMS takes the patient to a *non*–PCI-capable hospital, it is appropriate to consider emergency *interhospital transfer* of the patient to a primary PCI-capable hospital for mechanical revascularization if
  - Primary PCI has been determined to be the reperfusion modality of choice and can be initiated promptly within 90 minutes **from medical contact-to-balloon at the PCI-capable hospital,** OR

  - Fibrinolysis is administered and is unsuccessful, OR
  - There are contraindications to fibrinolysis

Patient Self-Transport (Discouraged)

- If fibrinolytic therapy has been determined to be the reperfusion modality of choice, the **door-to-needle** time should be within 30 minutes of arrival at the ED.
- If primary PCI has been determined to be the reperfusion modality of choice, and the patient arrives at a PCI-capable hospital, the **door-to-balloon** time should be within 90 minutes.
- If the patient presents to a non–PCI-capable hospital, it is appropriate to consider emergency *interhospital transfer* of the patient to a PCI-capable hospital if
  - Primary PCI is determined to be the reperfusion modality of choice and can be initiated within 90 minutes after the patient presented to the *initial* receiving hospital
  - Fibrinolysis is administered and is unsuccessful, OR
  - Fibrinolysis is contraindicated

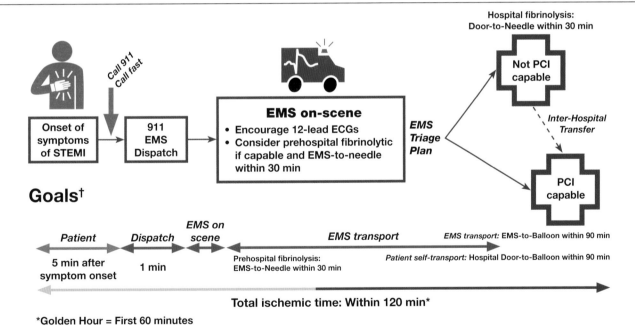

Figure 3. Options for EMS Transport of Patients with STEMI to Most Appropriate Facility.[22A,24]

*The medical system goal is to facilitate rapid recognition and treatment of patients with STEMI so that door-to-needle (or first medical contact–to-needle) for initiation of fibrinolytic therapy can be achieved within 30 minutes or door-to-balloon (or first medical contact–to-balloon) for PCI can be achieved within 90 minutes. These goals should not be understood as "ideal" times but rather the longest times that should be considered acceptable for a given system. Systems that are able to achieve even more rapid times for treatment of patients with STEMI should be encouraged. Note "first medical contact" is defined as "time of EMS arrival on scene" after the patient calls EMS/911 or "time of arrival at the emergency department door" (whether PCI-capable or non–PCI-capable hospital) when the patient transports himself/ herself to the hospital.

†EMS Arrival → Transport to non–PCI-capable hospital → Arrival at non–PCI-capable hospital to transfer to PCI-capable hospital → Arrival at PCI-capable hospital-to-balloon time-90 minutes. EMS indicates emergency medical system; PCI, percutaneous coronary intervention; and STEMI, ST-segment elevation myocardial infarction. Modified with permission.[23]

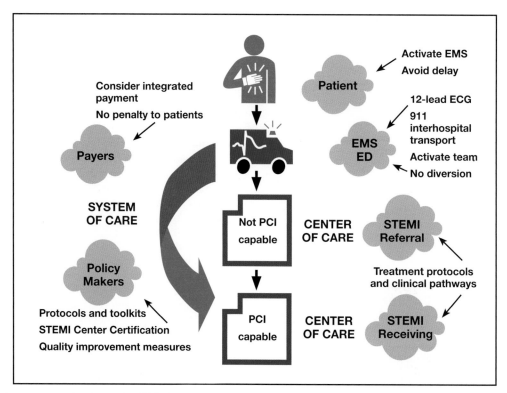

Figure 4. Improving access to timely care for STEMI patients: the ideal system. The core components involve a central focus on the patient, EMS, and hospital acute coronary care components. Other stakeholders involve "off-line" participants who facilitate and impact on the system, including physicians, third-part payers, and policy makers. From Jacobs et al.[25]

most benefit occurs in the first few hours, patients, family members, EMS personnel, and healthcare providers should operate with a sense of urgency—*time is muscle!* There are 3 major time intervals from the onset of ACS symptoms to the delivery of reperfusion therapy that provide opportunity for delay in treatment:

- Symptom onset to patient recognition and decision to act: accounts for 60% to 70% of delay
- Prehospital assessment, treatment, and transport: 5%
- Interval from ED arrival to reperfusion treatment: 25% to 35%

Patient delay, the interval from the onset of symptoms to the patient's recognition of them, accounts for 60% to 70% of the delay to definitive therapy.[26] *EMS transport* accounts for the least amount of delay, and prehospital notification of ACS patients can speed the diagnosis and reduce the time to reperfusion. Over the past decade many EDs have reduced the average time from ED arrival to administration of fibrinolytics through education, improved patient triage, and development of multidisciplinary protocols.

Reducing Patient Delays

Unfortunately the majority of patients still arrive by private vehicle and not EMS.[20,27] Timely access to the other components of the STEMI system of care requires that the patient recognize and activate the EMS system. EMS

system access with prearrival hospital notification and 12-lead ECG has been shown to speed the diagnosis of STEMI and decrease time to fibrinolytic therapy.[20,28-31]

Factors Associated With Delay

Chest discomfort is the major symptom in most patients (both men and women) with acute coronary syndromes. But patients frequently deny or misinterpret this and other symptoms. The elderly, women, and diabetic patients are most likely to delay, in part because they are more likely to have atypical symptoms or presentations. In the US Rapid Early Action for Coronary Treatment (REACT) trial,[32] the median prehospital delay was 2 hours or longer in non-Hispanic blacks, the elderly and disabled, homemakers, and Medicaid recipients. The decision to use an ambulance was an important variable that reduced prehospital delay; this reduction persisted after correction for variables associated with severity of symptoms. Other factors that can affect the interval between symptom onset and presentation to hospital include time of day, location (eg, work or home), and presence of a family member.

Patient Education

Education of patients with known coronary artery disease appears to be the only effective primary intervention to reduce denial or misinterpretation of symptoms. Clinical trials have shown that it is possible to increase awareness of MI symptoms and the need for EMS access through special educational programs.[20,33,34] Although public educational programs have had only transient effects and results have been difficult to sustain over time, implementing an educational science-based program such as the National Heart, Lung and Blood Institute's *Act in Time to Heart Attack Signs* is prudent in a comprehensive STEMI system of care (Figure 5). The physician and family members of patients with known coronary disease should reinforce the need to seek medical attention when symptoms recur because these patients paradoxically present later than patients with no known disease. Patients with known coronary disease should also be encouraged to use their nitroglycerin and activate EMS if symptoms persist or worsen 5 minutes after using the **first** nitroglycerin dose.

Reducing EMS Delays

Many factors have an impact on an optimal STEMI system of care and access to timely reperfusion. Evidence from multiple randomized trials suggests that primary percutaneous coronary intervention (PPCI) is superior to fibrinolytic therapy in reducing the rates of death, reinfarction, intracranial bleeding, reocclusion of the infarct related artery, and recurrent ischemia (even with interhospital transport) when performed in a timely fashion by experienced personnel.[35-37] However, not all hospitals are capable of performing primary percutaneous coronary intervention (PPCI). It is estimated that there are about 5000 acute care hospitals in the United States, and 2200 of these have cardiac catheterization capabilities. However, only 1200 of these are PPCI capable with the ability to acutely reperfuse an occluded coronary artery.[38] Systems should have the capability to determine which patients can benefit by rapid access to PPCI facilities with high volume skilled operators and cath lab personnel. When these criteria are met, PPCI is the preferred reperfusion modality for STEMI. Preferably,

STEMI systems of care should identify patients who can be taken primarily to PPCI centers and rapidly reperfuse those patients eligible for fibrinolytic therapy in non-PPCI centers or prehospital if transport is prolonged or delayed.

EMS Hospital Destination Protocols
Prehospital Triage and Interfacility Transfer

A STEMI triage system generally uses two models: pre-hospital triage versus interhospital transfer. The prehospital triage system transports patients directly to a regional or designated PPCI center and bypasses hospitals without PPCI capability. The interhospital transfer model takes patients to the nearest facility. Often treatment with fibrinolytics is considered and patients who are not eligible for pharmacological therapy and those with high risk MI are then transferred to regional PPCI centers. Both scene and interhospital transfer of patients with STEMI has been evaluated and found safe and efficient when integrated into a system of care.[39-43] One consideration in many systems is transport time to a PPCI capable facility. Survey's currently show that 80% of the adult population live within a 60-minute drive of a PPCI capable hospital and only 5% live further than 90 minutes from one.[44] One system in Ottawa, Canada with a single PPCI center and 4 non-PCI centers within a 7-mile radius, door-to-balloon times were 69 minutes when a paramedic interpreted the prehospital ECG and transported STEMI patients directly to the PPCI facility compared to 123 minutes when the ECG was not performed and the patient was initially brought to a non-PPCI facility and then transferred.[45]

Every community should have a written protocol that guides EMS system personnel where to take patients with possible STEMI. Patients in cardiogenic shock or with a large MI and a high risk of complications should be taken primarily or transferred secondarily to a regional facility with PPCI and cardiac surgical capabilities. The goal for the initiation

Foundation Facts	Evidence from multiple randomized trials suggests that primary percutaneous coronary intervention (PPCI) is superior to fibrinolytic therapy in reducing the rates of death, reinfarction, intracranial bleeding, reocclusion of the infarct related artery and recurrent ischemia (even with interhospital transport) when performed in a timely fashion by experienced personnel.[35-37]
FYI **ACC AHA STEMI Guidelines** **PCI for Patients With Cardiogenic Shock or Large MI**	Patients in cardiogenic shock or with a large MI and a high risk of dying should be taken primarily or transferred secondarily to an experienced PPCI facility. • The goal for interfacility transfer is a door-to-departure time within 30 minutes.[23]

Act in Time to
Heart Attack Signs

Use the T.I.M.E. Method To Help Your Patients Make a Heart Attack Survival Plan

Why Your Patients Need To Act in Time to Heart Attack Signs

Coronary heart disease is the leading killer of both men and women in the United States. Each year, about 1.3 million Americans suffer a heart attack. About 133,000 of those heart attacks are fatal. Disability and death from heart attack can be reduced with prompt thrombolytic and other artery-opening therapies–ideally given within the first hour after symptom onset. Patient delay is the largest barrier to receiving therapy quickly.

Heart Attack Warning Signs

▲ **Chest discomfort** (pressure, squeezing, fullness, or pain in the center of the chest)
▲ **Discomfort in one or both arms, back, neck, jaw, or stomach**
▲ **Shortness of breath** (often comes with or before chest discomfort)
▲ **Breaking out in a cold sweat, nausea, or light-headedness**

Uncertainty Is Normal

Most people think a heart attack is sudden and intense, like a "movie heart attack." The fact is that many heart attacks start slowly as mild pain or discomfort. People who feel such symptoms may not be sure what is wrong.

Delay Can Be Deadly

 Most heart attack victims wait 2 or more hours after symptoms begin before they seek medical help. People often take a wait-and-see approach or deny that their symptoms are serious. Every minute that passes without treatment means that more heart muscle dies.

Calling 9-1-1 Saves Lives

Minutes matter. Anyone with heart attack symptoms *should not wait more than a few minutes– 5 minutes at most–to call 9-1-1.*

Use the T.I.M.E. Method:

Talk with your patients about—
▲ Risk of a heart attack.
▲ Recognition of symptoms.
▲ Right action steps to take/rationale for rapid action.
▲ Rx–give instructions for when symptoms occur (based on patient history).
▲ Remembering to call 9-1-1 quickly– within 5 minutes.

Investigate—
▲ Feelings about heart attack.
▲ Barriers to symptom evaluation and response.
▲ Personal and family experience with AMI and emergency medical treatment.

Make a plan—
▲ Help patients and their family members to make a plan for exactly what to do in case of heart attack symptoms.
▲ Encourage patients and their family members to rehearse the plan.

Evaluate—
▲ The patient's understanding of risk in delaying.
▲ The patient's understanding of your recommendations.
▲ The family's understanding of risk and their plan for action.

Additional Resources

Find information and educational materials at the National Heart, Lung, and Blood Institute Web site: www.nhlbi.nih.gov and the American Heart Association Web site: www.americanheart.org

NATIONAL INSTITUTES OF HEALTH
NATIONAL HEART, LUNG, AND BLOOD INSTITUTE

Figure 5. Act in Time to Heart Attack Signs. Produced by the National Heart, Lung, and Blood Institute as part of the National Institutes of Health and the US Department of Health and Human Services.

of interfacility transfer is a door-to-departure time within 30 minutes.

Special Considerations

Patients in cardiogenic shock benefit from aggressive therapy, including intra-aortic balloon pump and percutaneous or surgical revascularization, when this can be accomplished within 36 hours of onset of MI and 18 hours from onset of shock.[15,46] Patients in cardiogenic shock on presentation should be taken primarily or transferred secondarily to a PPCI facility.[23]

"Almost all regional acute coronary syndromes are caused by disruption of an atherosclerotic plaque, either plaque rupture or plaque erosion. The majority of these plaques are non-occlusive prior to disruption and cause no symptoms."

Definition and Spectrum of Acute Coronary Syndromes

The formation and accumulation of lipid and oxidative byproducts in an arterial wall is called atherosclerosis. When this deposit involves the coronary arteries, it is called coronary atherosclerosis. This process is gradual (Figure 6) and asymptomatic for the many years of pathological progression.[47]

Almost all regional acute coronary syndromes are caused by disruption of an atherosclerotic plaque, either plaque rupture or plaque erosion. Many of these disruptions are subclinical events, but when symptoms occur a spectrum of clinical syndromes can result (Figure 7). These syndromes are unstable angina pectoris, non-ST-segment elevation myocardial infarction (NSTEMI) and ST-segment elevation myocardial infarction (STEMI). Sudden death can occur with any of these syndromes.

Development of Atherosclerosis and Vulnerable Plaque

Acute Coronary Syndrome

Secondary Prevention

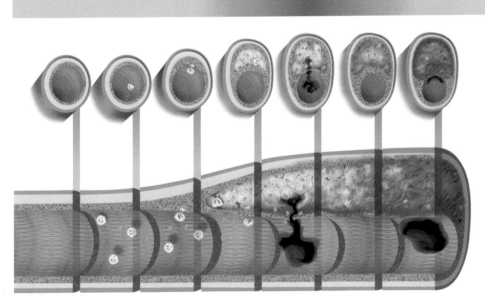

Figure 6. Chronological progression of plaque formation. The longitudinal section of an artery depicts the "timeline" of atherogenesis from a normal artery, to lesion initiation and accumulation of extracellular lipid in the intima, to lesion progression and weakening of the fibrous cap. An acute coronary syndrome develops when the vulnerable or high-risk plaque undergoes disruption of the fibrous cap, which is the stimulus for thrombogenesis. Modified from Libby.[47]

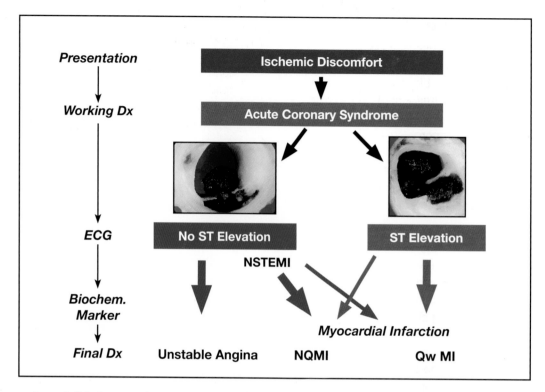

Figure 7. The spectrum of clinical presentations ranging from unstable angina through NSTEMI and STEMI are referred to as the acute coronary syndromes. Modified from Hamm CW, Bertrand M, Braunwald E. Acute coronary syndrome without ST elevation: implementation of new guidelines. *Lancet.* 2001;358:1533-1538, with permission from Elsevier; Davies MJ. The pathophysiology of acute coronary syndromes. *Heart.* 2000;83:361-366, with permission from BMJ Publishing Group Ltd.; and Alpert JS, Thygesen K, Antman E, Bassand JP. Myocardial infarction redefined—a consensus document of The Joint European Society of Cardiology/American College of Cardiology Committee for the Redefinition of Myocardial Infarction. *J Am Coll Cardiol.* 2000;36:959-969, with permission from the American College of Cardiology and the European Society of Cardiology.

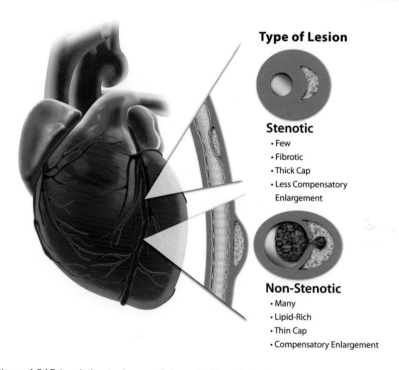

Type of Lesion

Stenotic
- Few
- Fibrotic
- Thick Cap
- Less Compensatory Enlargement

Non-Stenotic
- Many
- Lipid-Rich
- Thin Cap
- Compensatory Enlargement

Figure 8. Clinical manifestations of CAD in relation to degree of stenosis. Stenotic lesions tend to have smaller lipid cores, more fibrosis, and calcification; thick fibrous caps; and less compensatory enlargement (positive remodeling). They typically produce exertional ischemia when demand for coronary blood flow exceeds supply with exercise or emotion. Nonstenotic lesions generally outnumber stenotic plaques and tend to have large lipid cores and thin, fibrous caps susceptible to rupture and thrombosis. They often undergo substantial compensatory enlargement that leads to underestimation of lesion size by angiography. Nonstenotic plaques may cause no symptoms for many years but when disrupted can provoke an episode of unstable angina or MI.[48]

Stable and Unstable Plaques

Coronary atherosclerosis is a diffuse process with segmental lesions called *coronary plaques* that gradually enlarge and extend, causing variable degrees of coronary artery occlusion. Intravascular ultrasound of the coronary arteries has shown that the majority of the atheroma burden is subluminal and not visible by coronary angiography. Coronary arteries are usually closed about 70% (by angiography; 90% closed when viewed by a pathologist) before they cause symptoms and are considered for percutaneous coronary intervention or surgery (Figure 9, Stenotic Lesion).[49]

Most plaques do not cause symptoms and are non-occlusive. But nonocclusive plaques are the ones most prone to cause acute coronary syndromes (Figure 9, Nonstenotic Lesion). They have little hemodynamic effect before rupture, and stress testing and angiography cannot predict which ones will rupture and cause an ACS. Plaques can be classified as *stable* or *vulnerable* on the basis of their lipid content, thickness of the cap that covers and separates them from the arterial lumen, and the degree of inflammation in the plaque itself.

1. A **"stable"** intracoronary plaque (Figure 9A, Stenotic Lesion) has a lipid core separated from the arterial lumen by a thick fibrous cap. Stable plaques have less lipid, and the thick cap makes them resistant to fissuring and formation of thrombi. Over time the lumen of the vessel becomes progressively narrower, leading to flow limitations, supply-demand imbalance, and exertional angina. Stable plaques may progress to complete occlusion but do not usually cause STEMI because of the development over time of collateral supply to the myocardium at risk downstream from the lesion and preventing or limiting MI.

2. A **"vulnerable"** intracoronary plaque (Figure 9B, Non-Stenotic Lesion) has a lipid-rich core combined with an active inflammatory process that makes the plaque soft and prone to rupture. These plaques infrequently restrict blood flow enough to cause clinical angina, and functional studies (eg, stress tests) often yield negative results. Imaging techniques such as cardiac CT and magnetic resonance imaging are being investigated as tools to identify unstable and inflamed plaques and may be helpful in the future.

3. Inflammation is often found in the plaque. Inflammatory processes are concentrated in the leading edge impacted by coronary blood flow. It is here that most plaque ruptures occur. A plaque that is inflamed and prone to rupture is called **unstable** (Figure 9C).

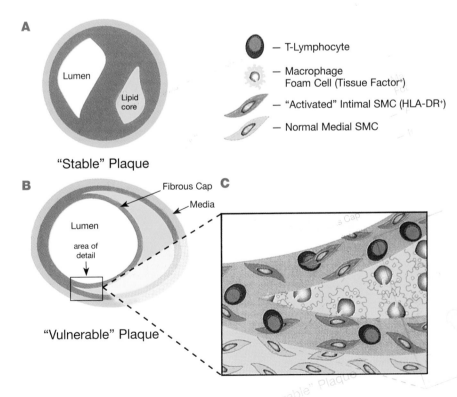

Figure 9. Stable and vulnerable plaques. **A,** Stable plaque. **B,** Vulnerable plaque. **C,** Area of detail of vulnerable plaque showing infiltration of inflammatory cells. SMC indicates smooth muscle cell. Reprinted from Libby P. Molecular bases of the acute coronary syndromes. *Circulation.* 1995;91:2844-2850.[49] © 1995 American Heart Association.

Progression to ACS

Triggers ACS/MI

Most episodes of ACS occur at rest or with modest daily activity. Heavy physical exertion or mental stress is present in a minority of patients, perhaps 10% to 15%.[50,51] Regular exercise appears to be protective and reduces the incidence of coronary events and sudden death, precipitated by exertion.[51-53] Conversely, individuals with low physical activity are at increased risk.[54]

There has been a documented circadian variation in the occurrence and presentation of acute coronary syndromes.[55] A diurnal pattern has been observed for AMI, ischemic episodes, sudden death, and stroke.[50,56-58] A peak incidence from 6:00 AM to noon has been noted, usually in the first 2 to 3 hours after arising.[59-61] Most likely the variation involves an interaction between the internal and external triggers of plaque instability, thrombosis, and ischemia.[62] There is an early morning increase in sympathetic activity accentuated by assumption of the erect posture. Coronary artery disease and abnormal endothelial responses appear to be a prerequisite for these factors to precipitate ACS.[63]

Plaque Rupture

When spontaneous or triggered plaque disruption occurs, a spectrum of pathological changes and intraluminal events occur that act in concert with platelet factors and the coagulation cascade to determine the clinical presentation. For example, if superficial erosion occurs in the setting of extracardiac stress, microemboli (Figure 10E) may result in elevation of cardiac troponin levels without manifest clinical symptoms (Figure 10A). Rupture of a coronary plaque (Figure 10B) can be asymptomatic, but if the resulting thrombus partially and intermittently occludes the epicardial coronary artery, unstable angina or NSTEMI occurs (Figure 10C). If the thrombus completely and persistently occludes the coronary artery, STEMI occurs and infarct size is determined by the amount of myocardium at risk, the degree and duration of occlusion, and the presence and extent of coronary collateral supply (Figure 10D).

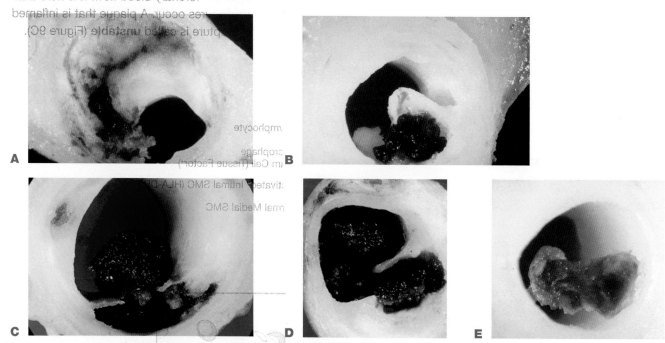

Figure 10. Coronary plaque disruption can result in several clinical outcomes. **A,** superficial erosion of a plaque has occurred but the coronary artery is patent. **B,** shows rupture of a coronary plaque that may progress to incomplete (**C**) or complete (**D**) coronary occlusion. In the acute coronary syndromes, emboli (**E**) from a disrupted plaque may lodge distal in the coronary tree and cause microvascular dysfunction in the absence of complete epicardial occlusion or after restoration of coronary patency. Figures courtesy of Professor Michael Davies, Guy's Hospital, London, England. Reproduced from Field JM. Pathophysiology and initial triage of acute coronary syndromes. In: Field JM, ed. *The Textbook of Emergency Cardiovascular Care and CPR.* Philadelphia, PA: Lippincott Williams & Wilkins; 2009:1-10; and Davies MJ. The pathophysiology of acute coronary syndromes. *Heart.* 2000;83:361-366, with permission from BMJ Publishing Group Ltd.

> *"When coronary artery plaque disruption occurs, a spectrum of clinical syndromes may result from unstable angina, non-ST-segment elevation MI, and ST-segment elevation MI. Sudden death can complicate any of these and may be the first, last and only symptom."*

Chest discomfort is the predominant symptom of ACS in both men and women. Chest discomfort of ischemic etiology is typically substernal and is often described as crushing, heavy, constricting, or oppressive. Symptoms suggestive of ACS include

- Uncomfortable pressure, fullness, squeezing, or discomfort in the center of the chest lasting several minutes (usually more than a few minutes)
- Chest discomfort spreading to the shoulders, neck, one or both arms, or jaw
- Chest discomfort spreading in the back or between the shoulder blades
- Chest discomfort with lightheadedness, fainting, sweating, or nausea
- Unexplained sudden shortness of breath with or without chest discomfort

Less commonly the discomfort occurs in the epigastrium and is described as indigestion. Just as a response to nitroglycerin is *not diagnostic* of cardiac ischemic pain, relief of pain with antacids in these patients is *not diagnostic* of a gastrointestinal cause.

Definition of Angina

Angina is a *symptom* often associated with chronic and gradual coronary artery narrowing. Classic stable angina is usually characterized by deep, poorly localized chest or arm discomfort. Stable angina is *reproducibly* associated with physical exertion or emotional stress and is *predictably* and promptly (<5 minutes) relieved with rest or sublingual nitroglycerin. Patients with chronic angina learn through experience how much physical exertion they can perform before the symptoms of angina begin. They also learn how soon and to what degree rest or nitroglycerin relieves the discomfort.

There are other causes of angina and symptoms may occur in the absence of coronary artery narrowing. Angina pectoris can share features with other conditions in the emergency differential diagnosis of chest discomfort and the symptom itself is not diagnostic of coronary artery disease. Unstable angina is broadly defined as a clinical syndrome falling between stable angina and acute MI in the spectrum of acute coronary syndromes. Most but not all patients with unstable angina will have coronary artery disease.

Classic angina is defined by 3 features
- Discomfort that is *squeezing, heavy, or tight.*
- The discomfort is precipitated by exertion or emotion.
- It is relieved by rest or nitroglycerin.

Typical and atypical chest discomfort
- Typical angina—all 3 features are present
- Atypical angina—only 2 features are present
- Atypical pain—1 or no features are present

Features not *characteristic* of myocardial ischemia
- Pleuritic pain
- Primary or sole location of discomfort in the middle or lower abdominal region
- Pain that can be localized by the tip of one finger
- Constant pain lasting for many hours or days
- Very brief episodes of pain lasting for a few seconds or less
- Pain that radiates into the extremities

Unstable Angina Pectoris

Unstable angina is an acute process of myocardial ischemia with insufficient severity and duration to cause myocardial necrosis. Patients with unstable angina typically do not

Critical Concept **Emergency Differential Diagnosis of Chest Discomfort**	Angina pectoris is a symptom and not a diagnosis because it may be caused by several conditions. There are 5 emergency differential diagnoses of angina and possible acute coronary syndromes: • Aortic dissection • Pulmonary embolism • Pericardial effusion with tamponade • Tension pneumothorax • Boerhaave's syndrome (esophageal rupture)

present with ST-segment elevation on the ECG and by definition do not release cardiac-specific biomarkers. Variations in terminology have been used in the past, originally when a change occurred in the predictable pattern of stable angina. These definitions have evolved over time, and unstable angina now indicates a period (usually over days or hours) of increasing symptoms precipitated by less exertion or prolonged episodes with minimal or no exertion. There are 3 principal presentations of unstable angina:

- **Rest angina:** Angina that occurs at rest, usually lasting less than 15 to 20 minutes.
- **Nocturnal angina:** Chest discomfort that awakens a patient at night.
- **Accelerating angina:** Previously diagnosed angina that is distinctly more frequent, longer in duration, or lower in threshold. *Threshold* is the level of activity (or class of angina) that induces pain or discomfort.

Myocardial Infarction

Angina—either stable or unstable—does not cause heart damage. But if the reduction in blood flow is prolonged or complete, heart cells (called myocytes) die. When this happens their internal cellular contents are released and can be detected in blood samples. This process usually takes 20 to 30 minutes or longer to begin. Myocyte death is called necrosis, and cardiac markers of necrosis that are often measured clinically are the MB isoenzyme of creatine kinase (CK-MB) and cardiac troponins. In contrast to more nonspecific changes of ischemia, infarction causes characteristic ECG changes. Myocyte necrosis can be due to any condition causing prolonged hypoxia to cardiac muscle (shock, cardiac arrest). The diagnosis of myocardial infarction due to ACS requires a positive biomarker and either clinical symptoms, imaging or pathological confirmation.

Sudden Cardiac Death

Acute ischemia or MI can cause electrical instability or catastrophic hemodynamic impairment. Sudden cardiac death results and is the major cause of out-of-hospital adult cardiac arrest in the hours after onset of symptoms. If an arrhythmia occurs as a primary event (not due to cardiogenic shock), *ventricular fibrillation* (VF) is the most

common presentation. Survival depends on many factors, including high-quality CPR, early defibrillation, and the presence of an underlying ACS. Resuscitation is more successful when VF occurs in the absence of an ACS, such as during cardiac rehabilitation or exercise stress testing.

Atypical Symptoms

Many patients with ACS do not present with the classic symptoms.[64] Women,[65-67] the elderly,[68] and insulin-dependent diabetics are especially prone to present with atypical symptoms. For this reason the "typical" ACS symptom *complex* is not a particularly sensitive indicator for ACS. In a large study of all patients presenting to an ED with "typical" ischemic symptoms, only 54% developed an ACS. In addition, the patients who did develop an ACS described a rich variety of symptoms: 43% had burning or indigestion, 32% had a "chest ache," and 20% had "sharp" or "stabbing" pain; 42% could not provide specific descriptors of their pain. The pain was partially pleuritic in 12%.[69]

The ACS symptom complex for women, the elderly, and diabetics may vary greatly. Chest discomfort or ache as the primary or chief symptom in itself may be minor. These patients may describe an ache or discomfort that may or may not be felt in the center of the chest but that seems to spread up to and across the shoulders, neck, arms, jaw, or back; between the shoulder blades; or into the epigastrium (upper left or right quadrant). The discomfort in the chest is less troublesome to the patient than the pain in the areas of radiation. This pattern of symptom localization *outside* the chest was found to be the most common atypical symptom of women evaluated in the Women's Ischemia Syndrome Evaluation (WISE) study.[70] The patient may be bothered more by associated lightheadedness, fainting, sweating, nausea, or shortness of breath. This is another example of the dominance of symptoms outside the chest. A global feeling of distress, anxiety ("something is wrong" or "something is just not right"), or impending doom may be present.

Women

Women presenting with MI typically present about 1 hour later than men, in part because of their atypical symptoms, which include epigastric pain, shortness of breath, nausea, and fatigue. Although women have a similar incidence of classic angina compared to men, significant CAD was present in the less than half of women in the angiographic substudy of the WISE trial.[71] In this study, 34% of the women referred for evaluation of ischemic pain had no detectable disease and 23% had measurable but minimal disease.

Several factors complicate evaluation of chest discomfort in women. Premenopausal women have a low likelihood of coronary artery disease (CAD) and commonly present with typical angina. The low incidence of positive angiograms in these women has led to a perception that their chest discomfort is benign and *nonischemic*. This misperception leads to underassessment of women with chest discomfort, so women with chest discomfort are less likely than men to be tested and treated for CAD. There is also a misperception that the course of CAD in women is more benign than it is in men. But the prognosis of women with CAD is similar to that of men, and women often have more angina and disability than men. Atypical symptoms in women often include the following:

- More angina at rest, occurring at night, or precipitated by mental rather than physical stress
- Shortness of breath, fatigue, palpitations, presyncope, sweating, nausea, or vomiting
- Atypical angina (in women with or without CAD)

Diabetics

Diabetic patients with ACS may present without chest discomfort but with complaints of weakness, fatigue, or severe weakness. Anginal equivalents such as shortness of breath, syncope, and lightheadedness may be their only symptoms. In diabetics with neuropathy these presentations have often been attributed to altered pain and neural perception.

Anginal Equivalents

Patients with ACS present with signs and symptoms that have been termed *ischemic equivalents or anginal equivalents*. It is important to note that these patients are *not* having atypical chest discomfort or pain as described above. These patients seldom offer complaints of "pain" in the chest, below the sternum, or elsewhere, and the healthcare provider may not be able to elicit a report of such pain or discomfort. Instead they may present with a symptom or sign that reflects the effects of the ischemia on left ventricular function or electrical stability of the heart. Diabetic patients and the elderly are most likely to present with these symptoms. With advancing age the elderly are more likely to present with diaphoresis. Some of the more common chest pain equivalent symptoms experienced by these ACS patients are

- Ischemic LV dysfunction: shortness of breath, dyspnea on exertion
- Ischemic arrhythmias: palpitations, lightheadedness or near-syncope with exercise, syncope

The most common signs of anginal equivalents are acute pulmonary edema or pulmonary congestion, cardiomegaly, and a third heart sound. Ventricular arrhythmias can cause symptoms in these patients. Ventricular extrasystoles, nonsustained ventricular tachycardia, and symptomatic ventricular tachycardia or ventricular fibrillation have been documented. Ventricular ectopy that *increases* with activity (most will suppress at increased sinus rates) is suspicious for ischemia. Atrial fibrillation is uncommonly an ischemic presentation. In most cases an anginal equivalent is diagnosed retrospectively when some objective evidence of ischemia has been linked to the patient's symptom complex. For example, left arm pain alone may raise suspicion of ACS in the appropriate clinical setting, but it is ischemic in origin only when definitely associated with ACS or reproduced with functional testing.

"Prehospital 12-lead ECGs and advance notification to the receiving facility speed diagnosis, shorten time to reperfusion, and may be associated with lower in-hospital mortality."

Initial EMS assessment and treatment involves identification of ischemic symptoms, performance of a 12-lead ECG and the initiation of immediate general treatment for ACS in appropriate patients.

Emergency Medical Dispatch

Emergency medical dispatchers and EMS providers must be trained to recognize symptoms of ACS. Dispatchers should advise patients with no history of aspirin allergy or signs of active or recent gastrointestinal bleeding to chew an aspirin (160 to 325 mg) while awaiting the arrival of EMS providers.[72,73]

Major EMS Assessments and Treatments (Box 2, Figure 11)

EMS system personnel in a STEMI system of care should be trained to

- Identify patients with acute ischemic chest pain or discomfort.
- Obtain an initial 12-lead ECG, provide pre-arrival notification to the receiving hospital, and transmit the ECG or their interpretation of the ECG to the receiving facility

- Obtain a targeted history with a fibrinolytic checklist to help determine eligibility for fibrinolytic therapy as appropriate
- Establish intravenous access and measure vital signs and oxygen saturation
- Start initial medical treatment (aspirin, nitroglycerin, and possibly oxygen and morphine)
- Document initial rhythms and prepare for treatment of ischemic arrhythmias, in particular VF/pulseless VT
- Place transcutaneous patches for transcutaneous pacing if symptomatic sinus bradycardia or advanced atrioventricular block occurs or may be anticipated

Recognition of Chest Discomfort Suggestive of Ischemia

A targeted history and physical examination are performed to aid diagnosis, evaluate and identify other causes of the patient's symptoms, and assess the patient for possible complications related to ACS or therapeutic interventions. Although the use of clinical signs and symptoms may increase suspicion of ACS, no single sign or combination of clinical signs and symptoms alone can confirm the diagnosis prospectively.[81-84] In addition, it is necessary to consider alternative life-threatening conditions as discussed above.

FYI **Guidelines 2010** **Dispatch Recommendations**	Dispatchers must be trained to recognize ACS symptoms. If authorized by medical control and protocol, dispatchers should advise patients with no history of aspirin allergy or signs of active or recent gastrointestinal bleeding to chew an aspirin (160 to 325 mg) while awaiting arrival of EMS providers.[72,73]

Critical Concept **Community EMS Priority**	Half of the patients who die of an ACS die before reaching the hospital. VF or pulseless VT is the precipitating rhythm in most of these deaths.[74-76] VF is most likely to develop during the first 4 hours after symptom onset.[7,77-79] Communities should develop programs to respond to out-of-hospital cardiac arrest that include recognition of ACS symptoms, activation of the EMS system, and availability of high-quality CPR and an AED.[80] EMS and dispatch system personnel should be trained to respond to cardiovascular emergencies.

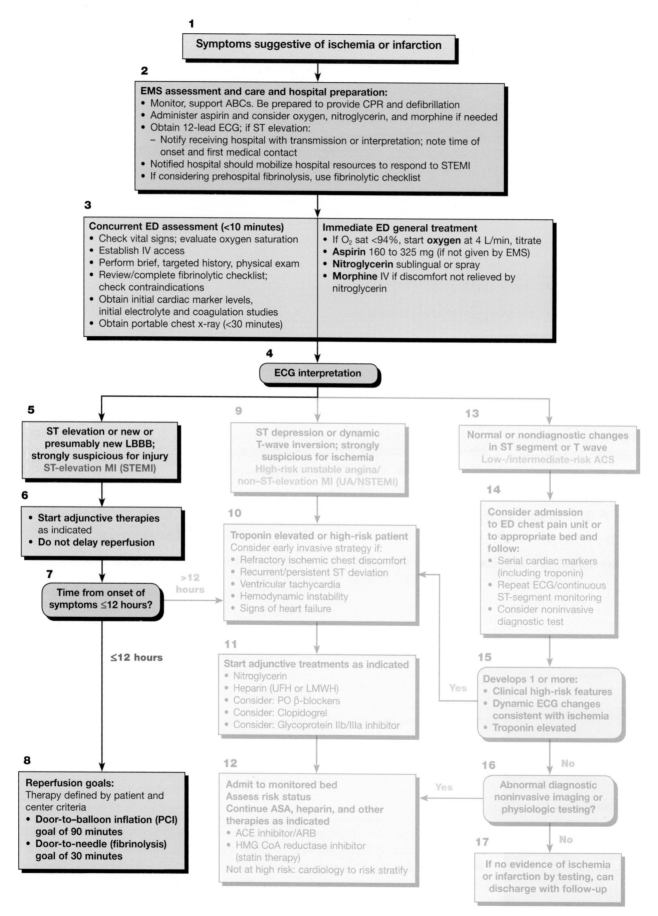

1
Symptoms suggestive of ischemia or infarction

2
EMS assessment and care and hospital preparation:
- Monitor, support ABCs. Be prepared to provide CPR and defibrillation
- Administer aspirin and consider oxygen, nitroglycerin, and morphine if needed
- Obtain 12-lead ECG; if ST elevation:
  – Notify receiving hospital with transmission or interpretation; note time of onset and first medical contact
- Notified hospital should mobilize hospital resources to respond to STEMI
- If considering prehospital fibrinolysis, use fibrinolytic checklist

3
Concurrent ED assessment (<10 minutes)
- Check vital signs; evaluate oxygen saturation
- Establish IV access
- Perform brief, targeted history, physical exam
- Review/complete fibrinolytic checklist; check contraindications
- Obtain initial cardiac marker levels, initial electrolyte and coagulation studies
- Obtain portable chest x-ray (<30 minutes)

Immediate ED general treatment
- If O₂ sat <94%, start **oxygen** at 4 L/min, titrate
- **Aspirin** 160 to 325 mg (if not given by EMS)
- **Nitroglycerin** sublingual or spray
- **Morphine** IV if discomfort not relieved by nitroglycerin

4
ECG interpretation

5
ST elevation or new or presumably new LBBB; strongly suspicious for injury ST-elevation MI (STEMI)

9
ST depression or dynamic T-wave inversion; strongly suspicious for ischemia High-risk unstable angina/ non–ST-elevation MI (UA/NSTEMI)

13
Normal or nondiagnostic changes in ST segment or T wave Low-/intermediate-risk ACS

6
- **Start adjunctive therapies** as indicated
- **Do not delay reperfusion**

10
Troponin elevated or high-risk patient
Consider early invasive strategy if:
- Refractory ischemic chest discomfort
- Recurrent/persistent ST deviation
- Ventricular tachycardia
- Hemodynamic instability
- Signs of heart failure

14
Consider admission to ED chest pain unit or to appropriate bed and follow:
- Serial cardiac markers (including troponin)
- Repeat ECG/continuous ST-segment monitoring
- Consider noninvasive diagnostic test

7
Time from onset of symptoms ≤12 hours?

>12 hours

≤12 hours

11
Start adjunctive treatments as indicated
- Nitroglycerin
- Heparin (UFH or LMWH)
- Consider: PO β-blockers
- Consider: Clopidogrel
- Consider: Glycoprotein IIb/IIIa inhibitor

15
Develops 1 or more:
- Clinical high-risk features
- Dynamic ECG changes consistent with ischemia
- Troponin elevated

Yes

8
Reperfusion goals:
Therapy defined by patient and center criteria
- **Door-to–balloon inflation (PCI) goal of 90 minutes**
- **Door-to-needle (fibrinolysis) goal of 30 minutes**

12
Admit to monitored bed
Assess risk status
Continue ASA, heparin, and other therapies as indicated
- ACE inhibitor/ARB
- HMG CoA reductase inhibitor (statin therapy)
Not at high risk: cardiology to risk stratify

16
Abnormal diagnostic noninvasive imaging or physiologic testing?

Yes

No

17
If no evidence of ischemia or infarction by testing, can discharge with follow-up

No

Figure 11. Acute Coronary Syndromes Algorithm—major EMS and ED assessments and treatment for STEMI.

Symptom Evaluation: Assess Life-Threatening Conditions

During initial evaluation of a patient with chest discomfort, the healthcare provider attempts to assess and estimate the probability of life-threatening problems in the differential diagnosis. But none of these life threats can be "ruled out" with absolute confidence during initial triage and evaluation. This fact underscores an important point: *healthcare providers should focus on both risk stratification and continuing assessment and diagnosis during initial patient evaluation.* As the evaluation proceeds and an initial strategy is defined, the risks and benefits of testing and treatment are balanced against the probability and risk assessment of disease using clinical judgment and prudent assessment.

Healthcare providers initially use symptoms to estimate the likelihood of ACS and to assess the probability of other life-threatening causes of chest discomfort. A differential diagnosis is developed and the probability of ACS and other life-threatening causes of chest discomfort is prioritized (Table 2). In the out-of-hospital setting this evaluation usually focuses on the symptom of chest discomfort and the 12-lead ECG can help identify patients with STEMI immediately despite symptom variability.

Table 2. Immediately Life-Threatening Causes of Chest Pain or Discomfort

- Acute coronary syndromes
- Aortic dissection
- Pulmonary embolism
- Pericardial effusion with acute tamponade
- Tension pneumothorax

Prehospital ECGs

Prehospital 12-lead ECGs and advance notification to the receiving facility speed diagnosis, shorten time to reperfusion, and may be associated with lower in-hospital mortality.[85-102] The reduction in door-to–reperfusion therapy interval in studies ranges from 10 to 60 minutes, but shorter times are possible when the cardiac catheterization laboratory is also activated.[103-109] EMS providers can efficiently acquire and transmit diagnostic-quality ECGs to

the ED[110-115] with a minimal increase in the on-scene time interval (0.2 to 5.6 minutes).[30,87,88,110,112,113,118-124]

Approximately 90% of EMS systems in a survey of US large cities had the capability to perform 12-lead ECGs.[116] Despite this, prehospital 12-lead ECGs are underutilized. They were obtained in only 5% of patients with STEMI during the period from 1994 to 1996[85] and 10% from 2000 to 2002.[86] In addition, even when a prehospital ECG is obtained the system often does not translate the information into effective actions required to shorten time to reperfusion.[86] There are some dedicated STEMI systems which have a demonstrated higher levels of use. For example, in North Carolina, prehospital 12-lead ECGs are obtained in 61% and 43% of STEMI patients transported to PCI and non-PCI centers, respectively.[117]

Several studies have examined the feasibility and accuracy of EMS providers to obtain a diagnostic ECG and identify STEMI using a variety of methodologies. Algorithm interpretation, healthcare professional interpretation, and wireless transmission to a physician are all feasible.[91,108,125-133] Qualified and specially trained paramedics and nurses can accurately identify typical ST elevation (>1 mm in 2 or more contiguous leads) in the 12-lead ECG with a specificity of 91% to 100% and a sensitivity of 71% to 97% (compared with emergency medicine physicians or cardiologists) and can provide advance notification by radio or cell phone to the receiving hospital.[91,134,135] There is good agreement with EMS providers and emergency department physician's interpretations.[91,136-138] Wireless transmission is possible, but transmission failures can occur in 20% to 44% of cases where wireless dead zones occur.[125,130,139-141] Ultimately, each STEMI system will be required to define the optimal method for integration of the ECG using available resources and personnel.

But performance of a prehospital ECG alone may not reduce or achieve optimal reductions in total ischemic time. For example, despite obtaining prehospital ECGs in 59% of patients at baseline, Sholz demonstrated a *reduction* in scene time from 25 to 19 minutes, ED evaluation from 14 to 3 minutes, door-to-balloon time 56 to 26 minutes and arterial access to balloon time 54 to 26 minutes when systematic quarterly feedback on performance was provided to all stakeholders including EMS. In aggregate, the performance of prehospital ECGs increased from 59% to 86%, on-scene time was decreased and total ischemic time reduced from

Foundation Facts

Prehospital ECGs and Receiving Facility Notification

- Transmission of the 12-lead ECG or interpretation and advance notification is recommended for patients exhibiting signs and symptoms of ACS.
- A prehospital 12-lead ECG with advanced ED notification may benefit patients with STEMI by reducing their time to reperfusion therapy.

113 to 74 minutes, a reduction of 39 minutes.[142] Remarkably, the number of patients handed off directly by the emergency physician to the interventional cardiologist increased from 23% during the first quarter of the study to 50%, 68%, and 76% during the second, third, and fourth quarters of the study.

If EMS providers identify STEMI on the ECG, it is reasonable for them to begin assessment of the patient for fibrinolytic therapy (ie, the fibrinolytic checklist, Figure 12).

Rapid Response Interventions *Destination Hospital Protocol for Cardiogenic Shock*	When possible, transfer patients with STEMI at high risk for mortality or severe LV dysfunction with signs of shock, pulmonary congestion, heart rate >100 *and* SBP <100 mm Hg to a facility capable of performing cardiac catheterization and rapid revascularization (PCI or CABG). • Also consider triage or transfer of patients with a large anterior wall infarct, congestive heart failure, or pulmonary edema. • Defer fibrinolytic therapy if PCI is *rapidly* available and anticipated first medical contact–to–balloon inflation time is ≤60 minutes. If you cannot ensure transfer within a time that would allow rapid PCI, administer fibrinolytics if there are no contraindications to their use. Then transfer the patient with a door-to-departure time of 30 minutes or less.

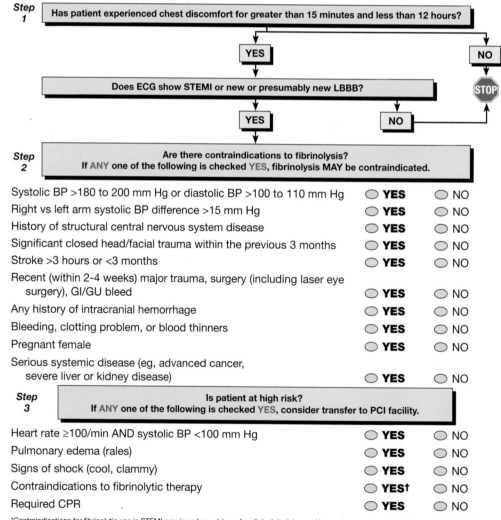

Prehospital Fibrinolytic Checklist*

Step 1 — Has patient experienced chest discomfort for greater than 15 minutes and less than 12 hours?

YES / NO

Does ECG show STEMI or new or presumably new LBBB?

YES / NO → STOP

Step 2 — Are there contraindications to fibrinolysis? If ANY one of the following is checked YES, fibrinolysis MAY be contraindicated.

Systolic BP >180 to 200 mm Hg or diastolic BP >100 to 110 mm Hg	◯ YES	◯ NO
Right vs left arm systolic BP difference >15 mm Hg	◯ YES	◯ NO
History of structural central nervous system disease	◯ YES	◯ NO
Significant closed head/facial trauma within the previous 3 months	◯ YES	◯ NO
Stroke >3 hours or <3 months	◯ YES	◯ NO
Recent (within 2-4 weeks) major trauma, surgery (including laser eye surgery), GI/GU bleed	◯ YES	◯ NO
Any history of intracranial hemorrhage	◯ YES	◯ NO
Bleeding, clotting problem, or blood thinners	◯ YES	◯ NO
Pregnant female	◯ YES	◯ NO
Serious systemic disease (eg, advanced cancer, severe liver or kidney disease)	◯ YES	◯ NO

Step 3 — Is patient at high risk? If ANY one of the following is checked YES, consider transfer to PCI facility.

Heart rate ≥100/min AND systolic BP <100 mm Hg	◯ YES	◯ NO
Pulmonary edema (rales)	◯ YES	◯ NO
Signs of shock (cool, clammy)	◯ YES	◯ NO
Contraindications to fibrinolytic therapy	◯ YES†	◯ NO
Required CPR	◯ YES	◯ NO

*Contraindications for fibrinolytic use in STEMI are viewed as advisory for clinical decision making and may not be all-inclusive or definitive. These contraindications are consistent with the 2004 ACC/AHA Guidelines for the Management of Patients With ST-Elevation Myocardial Infarction.

†Consider transport to primary PCI facility as destination hospital.

Figure 12. Fibrinolytic checklist.

Immediate General Treatment

Four agents are routinely recommended for immediate general treatment of patients with possible ischemic-type chest pain or discomfort unless allergies or other contraindications exist:

- **Oxygen** (if needed to maintain SpO$_2$ ≥94%)
- **Aspirin** 160 to 325 mg
- **Nitroglycerin** sublingual tablet or spray
- **Morphine** IV 2 to 4 mg if chest discomfort is unrelieved by nitrates

Immediate Pain Relief

Rationale

Healthcare professionals must place a high priority on alleviating acute ischemic pain during immediate general treatment. Ischemic pain produces complex neurohumoral activation, which in turn induces a heightened, anxiety-generating catecholamine state. As a result ischemic pain intensifies myocardial oxygen demand by accelerating heart rate, raising systolic blood pressure (SBP), and increasing contractility. This increased myocardial oxygen demand worsens existing ischemia and further impairs marginal hemodynamics.

Acute relief of pain will:

- Reduce myocardial oxygen demand (morphine, nitrates, β-blockers in some patients if not contraindicated)
- Attenuate the hyperactive catecholamine state (β-blockers)
- Reduce anxiety (morphine)

Oxygen (If Needed to Maintain SpO$_2$ ≥94%)

Rationale

Many patients with AMI (up to 70% in the first 24 hours[143]) demonstrate hypoxemia, due to either ventilation-perfusion mismatch or subclinical pulmonary edema from LV dysfunction. Experimental studies in animals have shown that oxygen administration can reduce ST elevation in anterior infarction.[144,145]

The effects of hypoxemia and respiratory insufficiency on a heart already compromised by coronary occlusion can be profound. Increased oxygen demand in a heart with marginal blood flow and reduced oxygen supply can lead to increased infarct size and cardiovascular collapse. It is difficult, however, to document the effects of oxygen on morbidity or mortality. A small double-blind clinical trial in which investigators randomly assigned 200 patients to room air or oxygen by mask found no difference in mortality, incidence of arrhythmias, or use of pain medications. No clinical studies, including one prospective, randomized, controlled trial and a recent clinical trial evaluating hyperbaric oxygen, have shown a reduction in morbidity, mortality, or complications due to arrhythmias with routine use of supplementary oxygen. The AMIHOT I trial demonstrated that intracoronary hyperoxemic reperfusion was safe and feasible, but failed to improve regional wall motion, ST-segment resolution, and final infarct size, except in a subgroup of anterior infarctions.[146] Supplementary oxygen has been shown to limit ischemic myocardial injury in animals,[144,147-149] but evidence of benefit in human trials is limited.[144] A case study found improvements in ST changes with the use of oxygen in humans.[150] Others suggested harm with low-flow oxygen administration.[143,151]

Recommendations

There is insufficient evidence to support routine use of oxygen in uncomplicated ACS. If the patient is dyspneic, hypoxemic, or has obvious signs of heart failure, providers should titrate therapy, based on monitoring of oxyhemoglobin saturation, to ≥94%.

Aspirin

Rationale

Administration of aspirin has been associated with reduced mortality in clinical trials, and multiple trials support the safety and efficacy of aspirin. Unless a true aspirin allergy or a recent history of gastrointestinal bleeding is present, aspirin should be given to all patients with possible ACS.

Critical Concept *Pain Relief and STEMI*	Relief of pain is an important early goal for patients with STEMI or another ACS. Surges of catecholamines have been implicated in - Plaque fissuring - Thrombus propagation - Reduction in VF threshold
Guidelines 2010 *Oxygen*	Administer oxygen to - All patients with evidence of respiratory compromise - Patients with oxygen saturation <94% Oxygen therapy should be titrated to SpO$_2$ ≥94%.

A dose of 160 to 325 mg aspirin causes immediate and near-total inhibition of thromboxane-A_2 production by inhibiting platelet cyclooxygenase (COX-1). Platelets are one of the principle and earliest participants in thrombus formation. This rapid inhibition also reduces coronary reocclusion and other recurrent events independently after fibrinolytic therapy. Platelet inhibitors are central to the prevention of acute stent thrombosis after placement in a coronary artery. The importance of aspirin was demonstrated in early fibrinolytic trials.

Aspirin alone reduced death from MI in the Second International Study of Infarct Survival (ISIS-2), and its effect was additive to the effect of streptokinase.[152] Clot lysis by fibrinolytics exposes free thrombin, a known platelet activator. Thus an antiplatelet effect is needed when fibrinolytic agents are administered. Patients can develop a paradoxical procoagulable state with fibrinolytic therapy unless platelet aggregation is reduced. In a review of 145 trials involving aspirin, investigators from the Antiplatelet Trialists' Collaboration reported a reduction in vascular events from 14% to 10% in patients with AMI. In high-risk patients aspirin reduced nonfatal AMI by 30% and vascular death by 17%.[153]

Recommendations for Initial Administration

- Administer aspirin to all patients initially suspected of having an acute ischemic syndrome.
- Have the patient chew a dose of 160 to 325 mg.
- Other formulations (soluble, IV) may be as effective. Consider rectal suppositories (300 mg) for patients unable to chew or swallow oral aspirin.

Precautions and Contraindications

Aspirin is contraindicated if patients have a history of true aspirin allergy, such as urticaria (hives) or systemic anaphylactic reaction. Patients with significant allergies or asthma may have an aspirin allergy—remember to ask!

Many patients will say they are allergic to aspirin when in fact they have had aspirin intolerance or a "side effect" in the past. That is, they may have had indigestion, nausea, or gastrointestinal upset. There is a dose-dependent increase in GI bleeding. Although this may preclude aspirin use on a chronic basis or necessitate the addition of another medication for GI prophylaxis, it does not preclude the use of aspirin in this life-threatening situation. Carefully review the history and weigh the risks and benefits. In patients with a true aspirin allergy, clopidogrel (300 mg) may be substituted for aspirin.

Oral aspirin is relatively contraindicated for

- Patients with active peptic ulcer disease (use rectal suppositories)
- Patients with a history of intolerance to aspirin
- Patients with bleeding disorders or severe hepatic disease

Nitroglycerin SL Tablet or Spray

Rationale

Nitroglycerin is an effective analgesic for ischemic chest discomfort, and it has beneficial hemodynamic effects. The physiological effects of nitrates cause reduction in left and right ventricular preload through peripheral arterial and venous dilation. Nitroglycerin is an endothelium-independent vasodilator of the coronary arteries (particularly in the region of plaque disruption), the peripheral arterial bed, and venous capacitance vessels.

There is little evidence that nitroglycerin improves outcomes for patients with AMI.[154] With this in mind, carefully consider use of these agents, especially when low blood pressure precludes the use of other agents shown to be effective in reducing morbidity and mortality (eg, β-blockers and angiotensin-converting enzyme [ACE] inhibitors).

Recommendations for Initial Administration

Nitroglycerin sublingual tablets or spray is the initial drug of choice for ischemic chest discomfort. Nitroglycerin SL tablets or spray should be given to all patients with suspected ischemic chest discomfort unless contraindications are present.

Critical Concept

Patient Use of Nitroglycerin

Acute Chest Discomfort

Previously patients with acute (not chronic) chest discomfort were instructed to take 3 doses of nitroglycerin and contact EMS if symptoms persisted.

New guidelines recommend that healthcare providers instruct patients and family to activate EMS if symptoms persist or worsen **5 minutes after the first nitroglycerin dose.** These patients may have STEMI or prolonged ischemia and are at risk for sudden cardiac death.

Recommendations for Initial Administration

- Use nitroglycerin as the first drug (before morphine) to help relieve ischemic chest discomfort.
- Use 1 tablet (0.3 to 0.4 mg) SL or spray 1 metered dose (0.4 mg) under or onto the tongue; repeat 2 times at 5-minute intervals. Monitor clinical effects and blood pressure.

Precautions, Adverse Effects, and Contraindications

- **Recent phosphodiesterase inhibitor use.** If the patient has taken sildenafil or vardenafil (ie, for erectile dysfunction) within the previous 24 hours or tadalafil within 48 hours, nitrates may cause severe hypotension refractory to vasopressor agents.
- **Hypotension, bradycardia, or tachycardia.** Avoid use of nitroglycerin in patients with hypotension (SBP <90 mm Hg), marked bradycardia (heart rate <50 bpm), or tachycardia (>100 bpm).
- **Right ventricular (RV) infarction.** Use nitroglycerin with caution in patients with inferior wall MI with possible RV involvement. Patients with RV dysfunction and acute infarction are very dependent on maintenance of RV filling pressures to maintain cardiac output and blood pressure. Until a 12-lead ECG and right sided precordial leads are performed, it is prudent to avoid nitroglycerin

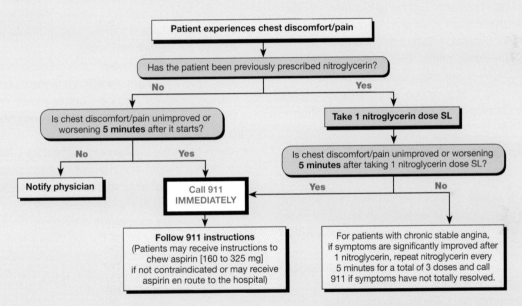

Treatment algorithm for potential STEMI patients who experience *non–trauma-related chest discomfort/pain.*

Patients *Without* Nitroglycerin Prescription

If patients have *not been previously prescribed nitroglycerin* (left side of algorithm), it is recommended that they call 911 if chest discomfort is unimproved or worsening 5 minutes after it starts. If the symptoms subside within 5 minutes of when they began, patients should notify their physician of the episode. For those patients with new onset chest discomfort who have not been prescribed nitroglycerin, it is appropriate to discourage them from seeking someone else's nitroglycerin (eg, from a neighbor, friend, or relative).

Patients *With* Nitroglycerin Prescription

If patients experience chest discomfort and *have been previously prescribed nitroglycerin* and have it available (right side of algorithm), it is recommended that they be instructed (in advance) to take 1 nitroglycerin dose immediately in response to symptoms. If chest discomfort/pain is unimproved or worsening 5 minutes after taking 1 nitroglycerin dose, it is recommended that the patient call 911 immediately to access EMS. If the symptoms disappear after taking 1 nitroglycerin dose, the angina management recommendations in the *ACC/ AHA Guidelines for the Management of Patients With Chronic Stable Angina* apply.

for patients with borderline low blood pressure (SBP ≤100 mm Hg) or borderline bradycardia (heart rate <60 per minute). Patients with excess vagal tone are unable to compensate when venodilation decreases blood pressure. Remember, cardiac output is the result of stroke volume and heart rate. If stroke volume falls because of decreased ventricular preload (caused by vasodilation), heart rate will be unable to compensate by increasing. Patients with a tachycardia may already be compensating (compensatory tachycardia) and unable to increase rate further. They also may become hypotensive. Although heart rates are listed in the guidelines (extreme bradycardia <50 per minute; tachycardia >100 per minute), these are not absolute, and the principles and clinical assessment further guide therapy around these heart rate limits.

- Transdermal preparations are generally avoided in potentially unstable patients; topical application results in variability in the amount of drug delivered and poorly predictable hemodynamic effect, and absorption is often erratic. The nitrate preparation is absorbed into the dermal skin layers and may not be completely removed by wiping to stop action. Avoid long-acting oral preparations, especially in patients who may become hemodynamically unstable.

Morphine Sulfate

Rationale

Morphine is the analgesic of choice for patients with ischemic pain unresponsive to nitrates. Morphine is an important treatment, particularly for STEMI, because complete coronary occlusion is often associated with a hyperadrenergic state. Surges of catecholamines have been implicated with plaque fissuring, thrombus propagation, and a reduction in VF threshold. Morphine has the following effects:

- Produces central nervous system analgesia, which reduces the toxic effects of neurohumoral activation, catecholamine release, and heightened myocardial oxygen demand
- Produces venodilation, which reduces LV preload and oxygen requirements

- Decreases systemic vascular resistance, thereby reducing LV afterload
- Helps redistribute blood volume in patients with acute pulmonary edema

Similar to nitroglycerin, morphine is a vasodilator and is not to be used in patients with suspected hypovolemia or inadequate right or left ventricular preload.

Precautions, Adverse Effects, and Contraindications

- Avoid morphine in patients who are hypotensive and in patients with suspected hypovolemia.
- Morphine-induced hypotension is secondary to its vasodilative properties; it most often develops in volume-depleted patients.
- If hypotension develops in a supine patient in the absence of pulmonary congestion, elevate the patient's legs and administer a normal saline bolus of 200 to 500 mL IV. Assess the patient frequently.
- Avoid concomitant use of other vasodilators, such as IV nitroglycerin, in patients with continued, unresponsive pain. A β-blocker may be a better choice than nitroglycerin for refractory ischemic pain, unless contraindications are present.
- The respiratory depression associated with morphine seldom presents a significant problem because the increased adrenergic state associated with infarction or pulmonary edema maintains respiratory drive.
  - If significant respiratory depression does occur, administer naloxone 0.4 mg IV at 3-minute intervals. Naloxone will reduce any morphine-induced respiratory depression that may occur. If hypoventilation persists, consider other causes.

Prehospital Fibrinolysis

Clinical trials have shown that the greatest potential for myocardial salvage comes from initiating fibrinolysis as soon as possible after the onset of ischemic-type chest discomfort. To reduce the time to treatment, a number of researchers have proposed and evaluated prehospital administration of fibrinolytics.

ACC/AHA STEMI Guidelines 2007 **Morphine**	**Dose Titration for Morphine** • Initial dose 2 to 4 mg • Incremental dose 2 to 8 mg at 5-minute to 15-minute intervals The 2004 ACC/AHA guidelines for management of STEMI[73] issued a concern for under-dosing patients with morphine and other analgesics. Pain, which is commonly severe early in STEMI, is associated with excess sympathetic activity and a hyperadrenergic state. Morphine is the agent of choice to treat this condition. Do not use pain relief or control to assess anti-ischemic or reperfusion therapy.

A meta-analysis of multiple prehospital fibrinolytic trials found a 17% relative improvement in outcome associated with prehospital fibrinolytic therapy.[155] The greatest improvement was observed when therapy was initiated 60 to 90 minutes earlier than in the hospital. More recently a meta-analysis evaluated time to therapy and impact of prehospital fibrinolysis on all-cause mortality.[156] Analysis of pooled results from 6 randomized trials with more than 6000 patients showed a significant 58-minute reduction in time to drug administration. This time reduction was associated with decreased all-cause hospital mortality. These studies concluded that out-of-hospital–initiated fibrinolytic therapy can definitely shorten the time to fibrinolytic treatment. These time savings can be offset whenever effective ED triage results in a door-to-drug time of 30 minutes or less, obviating the need for implementation of special training and a rigorous out-of-hospital protocol.[157]

More recent trials have continued to show a reduction in treatment time when fibrinolytics are administered before arrival at the hospital. The Assessment of the Safety and Efficacy of a New Thrombolytic Regimen trial (ASSENT III Plus) showed reduced treatment delay (40 to 45 minutes) but increased cerebral hemorrhage (in patients aged >75 years).[158] The Early Retavase–Thrombolysis in Myocardial Infarction (ER-TIMI 19) trial and the Comparison of Angioplasty and Prehospital Thrombolysis in Acute Myocardial Infarction (CAPTIM) trial evaluated prehospital fibrinolysis and demonstrated a consistent decrease in time to treatment.[14,159] In the CAPTIM trial no mortality difference

was noted when patients received either prehospital fibrinolytic therapy or PCI when therapy was initiated within 3 hours of symptom onset.

When prehospital personnel identify a patient with STEMI, it is appropriate for them to begin a fibrinolytic checklist when clinically indicated by protocol (Figure 12).

Destination Protocols

Prehospital Triage and Interfacility Transfer

Every community should have a written protocol that guides EMS system personnel where to take patients with possible STEMI. Patients in cardiogenic shock or with large MI and a high risk of dying should be taken primarily or transferred secondarily to a PCI facility. The goal for interfacility transfer is a door-to-departure time of 30 minutes or less.

Special Considerations

Patients in cardiogenic shock benefit from aggressive therapy, including intra-aortic balloon pump and percutaneous or surgical revascularization, when this can be accomplished within 36 hours of onset of MI and 18 hours from onset of shock. Patients in cardiogenic shock should be taken primarily or transferred secondarily to a PCI facility.

Foundation Facts
 	
Prehospital Fibrinolytic Therapy
	Establishment of a prehospital fibrinolysis program is reasonable in the following settings:
	
	1. EMS systems where physicians are present in the ambulance
	2. A well-organized EMS system with full-time paramedics and
	    • 12-lead ECGs with transmission capability
	    • Initial and ongoing ECG training for paramedics
	    • On-line medical command and a medical director with training and experience in STEMI management
	    • Ongoing continuous quality-improvement program
	
	When EMS has fibrinolytic capability and the patient qualifies for treatment, it is recommended that a fibrinolytic should be administered within 30 minutes of EMS arrival.

ACC/AHA STEMI Guidelines 2004 **PCI for Patients With Cardiogenic Shock or Large MI**	Patients in cardiogenic shock or with a large MI and a high risk of dying should be taken primarily or transferred secondarily to an experienced PCI facility. Given the importance of avoiding delays, direct transport to a facility is preferable. • The goal for interfacility transfer is a door-to-departure time of 30 minutes or less. • When a delay is unavoidable, fibrinolytic therapy is indicated in eligible patients

"The 12-lead ECG is central to the triage of patients with chest discomfort. A 12-lead ECG should be performed and shown to an experienced emergency physician within 10 minutes of ED arrival on all patients with suspected cardiac ischemia."

Early evaluation and management in the ED emphasizes efficient, focused evaluation of the patient with ischemic chest discomfort. The 4 "D's" of STEMI survival serve as benchmarks for time, evaluation, and treatment goals.

The 4 D's of STEMI Survival

Time is muscle. Limitation of infarct size historically relied on early reperfusion therapy with fibrinolytic drugs. Goals were developed on the basis of the open artery hypothesis— open the infarct-related artery, restore perfusion to the myocardium, limit infarct size, and reduce death and complications of MI (eg, congestive heart failure). The 4 D's represent benchmarks and time goals in the reperfusion strategy: **D**oor, **D**ata, **D**ecision, and **D**rug. The door-to– drug administration goal is 30 minutes although PCI is the preferred strategy if the door-to-balloon time is within 90 minutes.

Rapid STEMI ID, Triage and Treatment

The 12-Lead ECG in STEMI
(See also the section on 12-lead ECG analysis.)

The 12-lead ECG is central to the triage of patients with chest discomfort. A 12-lead ECG should be performed and shown to an experienced emergency physician within

10 minutes of ED arrival on all patients with suspected cardiac ischemia.

Inexperienced healthcare providers can learn to recognize certain ECG patterns and features with basic training and some clinical experience. Patterns of ST deviation allow the provider to recognize the presence of STEMI in most instances.

Basic ECG Measurements

Healthcare providers who may evaluate acute chest discomfort should be familiar with the basic concepts of ECG measurements and intervals from rhythm analysis. The ST segment is the cornerstone of decision making in the initial triage of patients into the 3 treatment categories. STEMI is emphasized in this manual because of the urgency of timely intervention needed to reopen the coronary artery.

Figures 13 and 14 demonstrate ST elevation. For more information on measuring ST elevation, see page 40.

Serial, Repeat, or Continuous 12-Lead ECGs?

If the initial ECG is nondiagnostic, serial ECGs are recommended. The clinician must determine the frequency of repeat ECGs, but perform at least 1 repeat ECG approximately 1 hour after the first. If the initial ECG is nondiagnostic but the patient is symptomatic and there is

Critical Concept **ECG Criteria for Fibrinolytic Therapy**	In addition to chest discomfort consistent with ongoing ischemia/infarction, the ECG must meet 1 of the following criteria to qualify the patient for acute reperfusion therapy: • ST-segment elevation in 2 or more contiguous leads; threshold values of 2 mm (0.2 mV) in leads V_2 and V_3* or 1 mm in all other leads • New or presumably new LBBB • ST-segment depression if criteria for true posterior MI are present *2.5 mm in men <40 years; 1.5 mm in all women.

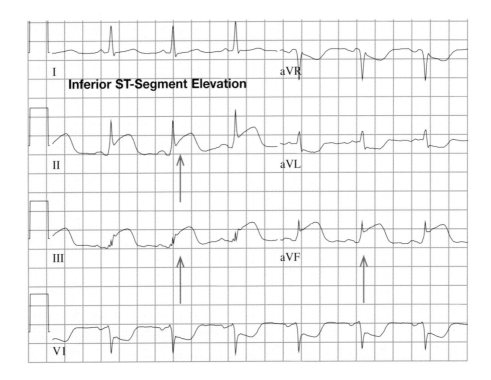

Figure 13. Leads II, III, and aVF from a 12-lead ECG demonstrate significant ST-segment elevation (red arrows) typical of STEMI. In this instance leads II, III, and aVF are contiguous inferior leads. A 12-lead ECG is required to confirm an inferior myocardial infarction.

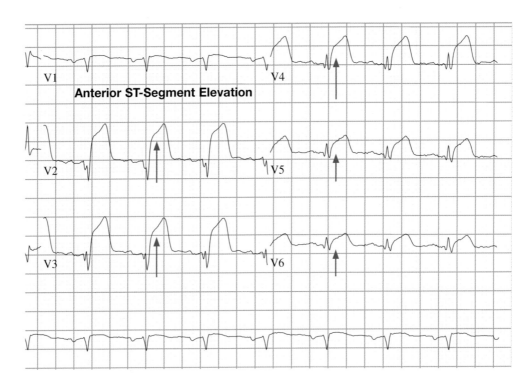

Figure 14. A 12-lead ECG demonstrating ST-segment elevation (blue arrows) in anterior leads V_2 through V_6, consistent with a large anterior wall myocardial infarction.

a high clinical suspicion for STEMI, obtain repeat ECGs at 5-minute to 10-minute intervals or initiate continuous 12-lead ST-segment monitoring.

Dynamic ECG Changes

Repeat or serial ECGs often show *dynamic 12-lead changes,* meaning that the ST changes on the initial ECG normalize or a nondiagnostic initial ECG becomes abnormal. For example, ST elevation shown on an initial 12-lead ECG obtained in a satellite clinic or by EMS personnel in the field may be resolved minutes later on the ED ECG. It would be a serious error to base further management on the normalized ECG rather than on the initial abnormal recording.

New or Presumably New LBBB?

A *new* left bundle branch block (LBBB) in the context of ischemic-like chest discomfort is an ominous event, indicating an occlusion in the left coronary artery system, usually above the septal branch of the left anterior descending artery. When an LBBB is present, the delayed LV depolarization of LBBB distorts the ST segment, preventing accurate identification of ST elevation. Thus the clinician operates without the ability to identify primary ST elevation. Because ST elevation has become the essential criterion for the use of fibrinolytics, its secondary repolarization change in patients with LBBB has posed difficulties in the many clinical trials of fibrinolytic therapy. In an excellent recent review of this problem, Kontos et al[160] observed that the fibrinolytic mega-trials were inconsistent and contradictory in regard to "new BBB." The trials used highly variable inclusion and exclusion criteria for chest discomfort patients presenting with "bundle branch block," "left bundle branch block," or "right bundle branch block."

Fibrinolytic trials have defined some changes in ECG morphology that increase the likelihood of MI in the presence of LBBB. But in most cases an experienced electrocardiographer is needed.

Determination of "New or Presumably New" LBBB

New or presumably new LBBB occurs in a about 10% of patients presenting with chest discomfort.[161] A determination of "new" LBBB requires copies or reports of previous ECGs that may be difficult or impossible to obtain expediently. This inability to determine whether the LBBB is old or new forces the clinician to use clinical judgment and consideration of the benefits versus the risks of fibrinolytic therapy. In this clinical situation most clinicians will weigh heavily on patient symptom onset, consistency with classic anginal symptoms, and the degree of severity in the final decision about therapy. In a decision analysis Gallagher[162] compared outcomes from a treatment strategy based on the ECG algorithm by Sgarbossa et al[163-165] with outcomes from a treatment strategy of simply giving fibrinolytics to all symptomatic patients with LBBB. The analysis intentionally ignored the question of "new versus old" BBB and concluded that fibrinolytic administration was appropriate for all patients with BBB and ischemic-like chest discomfort.[162]

Bundle Branch Block Obscuring ST-Segment Analysis and New RBBB

Bundle branch block obscuring ST-segment analysis and a history suggesting MI was one of the initial indications for fibrinolytic therapy[166] now replaced with new or presumably new LBBB.[23] However, patients with both LBBB and RBBB have lower rates of treatment with fibrinolytic therapy and with aspirin, nitrates, and β-blockers during the first 24 hours of admission, suggesting either left or right bundle branch block impedes identification and treatment of STEMI.[167] A new or presumably new right bundle branch block (RBBB) due to STEMI occurs in 10% to 15% of patients with AMI and is associated with increased mortality comparable to LBBB.[168-175]

Acute ST-segment changes are more readily identified with RBBB and should not be overlooked (Figure 15). LBBB affects the entire QRS complex, but RBBB obscures the terminal portion of the QRS complex. ST-segment changes suggestive of STEMI can be identified in most patients as well as significant or new Q waves. But any BBB that obscures ST-segment elevation in the setting of a high clinical suspicion of AMI may be an indication for reperfusion therapy. In NRMI-2 the presence of a new or presumably new RBBB had a 64% increased odds ratio for in-hospital death, and patients with LBBB had a 64% increased odds ratio for death compared to patients without BBB.[167] If fibrinolytic therapy is contraindicated, consider coronary angiography if suspicion remains high.

Cardiac Markers in STEMI

Previously called "cardiac enzymes," cardiac markers are released from myocytes undergoing necrosis. The clinical markers used today are predominantly the creatine kinase subform found predominantly in the heart (CK-MB) and the cardiac specific troponins (cTn). See Figure 16.

In many patients cardiac markers are not elevated within the first several hours after onset of chest discomfort. Because they may take 6 to 8 hours to reach detectable levels, cardiac markers are not used to identify patients with STEMI for reperfusion therapy.

STEMI—Adjunctive Therapy

After initial management and stabilization, additional drug therapy is administered. Although adjunctive therapy applies generally to many patients, the selection of drugs—and sometimes doses—is individualized on the basis of management strategies, local protocols, and the clinician's patient and data assessments. The following is an overview and is not to be viewed as routine recommendations or an in-depth discussion for patients with ACS or STEMI. In addition, this area is fluid and clinical trials continue to evolve. There is no substitute for a knowledgeable physician applying this data to individual patients at the bedside.

Intravenous Nitroglycerin

The outcome benefits of intravenous nitroglycerin are limited, and no conclusive evidence supports routine use of intravenous, oral, or topical nitrate therapy in patients with AMI.[154] With this in mind, carefully consider use of these agents, especially when low blood pressure precludes the use of other agents shown to be effective in reducing morbidity and mortality (eg, β-blockers and angiotensin-converting enzyme [ACE] inhibitors).

Recommendations for IV Administration

IV nitroglycerin is not used *routinely* in patients with STEMI. A pooled analysis of more than 80 000 patients showed only a possible small effect of nitrates on mortality (odds reduction 7.7% to 7.4%). Do not administer IV nitroglycerin when it precludes the use of agents shown to have a greater treatment effect for STEMI (β-blockers, ACE inhibitors). During initiation of therapy blood pressure should be carefully monitored and repeated before each dose titration.

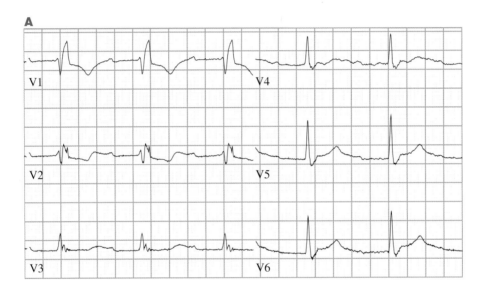

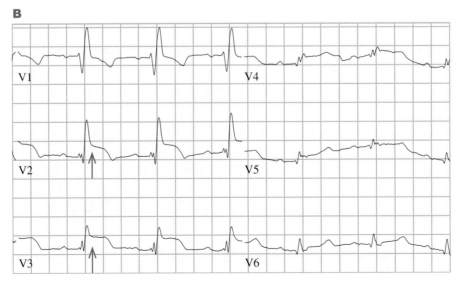

Figure 15. ECG leads V_1 through V_6 in patients with right bundle branch block. **A,** Patient with chest discomfort and right bundle branch block without STEMI by coronary angiography. Typical rSR' pattern in leads V_1 through V_2. **B,** Patient with occlusion of left anterior descending coronary artery. Note injury current in leads V_2 and V_3 (red arrows). If carefully examined, these ST-segment elevations can be overlooked or attributed to RBBB.

Dosing Recommendation for IV Nitroglycerin

The same cautions and contraindications exist for intravenous and oral nitrates. When intravenous nitrates are given, take care to frequently assess the patient and titrate the dose to avoid complications of therapy in the setting of STEMI/ACS. Drug-induced hypotension decreases coronary perfusion and microvascular flow and has the potential to increase ischemia.

- Check vital signs and heart rate for contraindications before starting and before each increase in dose

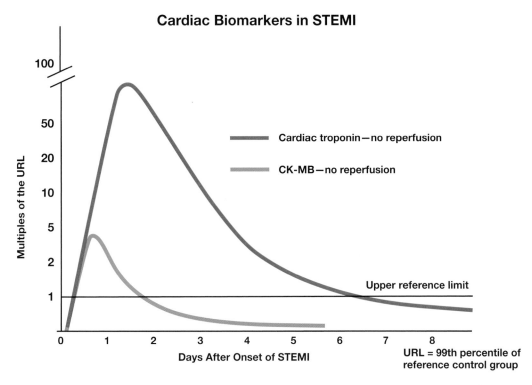

Cardiac Biomarkers in STEMI

Days After Onset of STEMI

Multiples of the URL

Cardiac troponin—no reperfusion

CK-MB—no reperfusion

Upper reference limit

URL = 99th percentile of reference control group

Figure 16. Cardiac biomarkers in STEMI.[176] Typical cardiac biomarkers that are used to evaluate patients with STEMI include the MB isoenzyme of CK (CK-MB) and cardiac-specific troponins. The horizontal line depicts the upper reference limit (URL) for the cardiac biomarker in the clinical chemistry laboratory. The URL is that value representing the 99th percentile of a reference control group without STEMI. The kinetics of release of CK-MB and cardiac troponin in patients who do not undergo reperfusion are shown. Adapted from Wu AH, Apple FS, Gibler WB, Jesse RL, Warshaw MM, Valdes R. National Academy of Clinical Biochemistry Standards of Laboratory Practice: recommendations for the use of cardiac markers in coronary artery diseases. *Clin Chem.* 1999;45:1104-1121,[177] with permission from American Association for Clinical Chemistry, Inc.

FYI Guidelines 2010 IV Nitroglycerin	STEMI Indications for IV Nitrates - Ongoing (after SL tablets or spray) or recurrent ischemic discomfort - Preferred agent for hypertension and STEMI/ACS - Adjunct to treat pulmonary congestion (congestive heart failure)
Dosing Regimen for IV Nitroglycerin	- Begin infusion at 10 mcg/min. - Increase dose by 10 mcg/min every 3 to 5 minutes until symptom or blood pressure response is noted. - A ceiling dose of 200 mcg/min is commonly used. - Systolic blood pressure (SBP) generally should not be reduced to less than 110 mm Hg in previously normotensive patients or 25% below the starting SBP in hypertensive patients. - Avoid nitroglycerin in SBP <90 mm Hg or 30 mm Hg or more below patient's baseline. - Avoid nitroglycerin if marked bradycardia or tachycardia exists.

β-Adrenergic Receptor Blockers

In-hospital administration of β-blockers may reduce the size of the infarct, incidence of cardiac rupture, and mortality in patients who do not receive fibrinolytic therapy.[178-182] This data was largely observed during clinical trials before the "reperfusion era." β-Blockers also reduce the incidence of ventricular ectopy and fibrillation.[183] A small but significant decrease in death and nonfatal infarction has been observed in patients treated with β-blockers very soon after the onset of symtpoms.[184]

Oral β-blockers should be administered for ACS of all types within 24 hours unless contraindications are present. It is reasonable to start oral β-blockers with low doses after the patient is stabilized prior to discharge. They should be given irrespective of the need for revascularization therapies. IV β-blockers have been administered in the ED based on the results from the Metoprolol in Acute Myocardial Infarction (MIAMI) trial, but they are not "routine" and they require risk stratification. In the reperfusion era early administration of β-blockers decreased recurrent ischemia but did not appear to have a mortality benefit. To assess modern use, the Clopidogrel and Metoprolol in Myocardial Infarction Trial (COMMIT CCS2) trial used the MIAMI dosing schedule, administering 3 doses of metoprolol 5 mg IV over 15 minutes[185] (Figure 17). In this large trial there was no benefit from early administration of IV β-blockers. An analysis of prespecified subgroups showed that about 10 lives per 1000 were saved by a reduction in VF and recurrent MI, but this benefit was offset by an increase in patient death from cardiogenic shock. Lives lost from cardiogenic shock increased with increasing Killip class, likely as a result of an increase in death from heart failure since LV dysfunction and CHF increases with infarct size. For this reason careful attention should be given to treating patients with congestive heart failure. A tachycardia in these patients may be compensatory as heart rate compensates for impaired and decreased stroke volume due to infarction.

Updated Recommendations

ACC/AHA Focused Update Guidelines for Management STEMI 2007

β-Adrenergic Blockade Early in STEMI

CAREFUL!

Oral β-Adrenergic Blockade Early in STEMI

Oral β-blockade should be initiated within first 24 hours in STEMI to patients not at high risk* without any of the following:

- Signs of heart failure
- Evidence of low output state
- Increased risk for cardiogenic shock
- Other relative contraindications

Patients with early contraindication to β-blockade should be reevaluated for candidacy for secondary prevention before discharge.

Patients with moderate to severe heart failure should receive β-blockade as secondary prevention with a gradual titration scheme.

IV β-Adrenergic Blockade Early in STEMI

Reasonable to administer IV β-blockade to patients who are *hypertensive* and who do not have

- Signs of heart failure
- Evidence of low output state
- Increased risk for cardiogenic shock*
- Other relative contraindications

IV β-blockade should not be administered to patients who have any of the following:

- Signs of heart failure
- Evidence of low output state
- Risk factors for cardiogenic shock*
- Other relative contraindications: PR interval >0.24 second- or third-degree AV block, active asthma or reactive airway disease

---

*Risk factors for cardiogenic shock include

- Age >70 years
- SBP <120 mm Hg
- Heart rate >110 or <60 per minute
- Delayed presentation

If initially contraindicated (see above), patients are serially reassessed for initiation of therapy before discharge. Oral β-blockers may need to be given in low and titrated doses after the patient is stabilized and acute heart failure has resolved. This approach permits earlier administration of ACE inhibitors (ACE-I), which are documented to reduce 30-day mortality rates (see below). ACE-I inhibitors are started after reperfusion and when the patient is hemodynamically stable. This will usually occur after transfer from the emergency department.

Heparins

Heparin is an indirect inhibitor of thrombin that has been widely used as adjunctive therapy for fibrinolysis and in combination with aspirin for the treatment of NSTEMI and unstable angina. Heparin is also used with PCI.

Unfractionated Heparin

Unfractionated heparin (UFH) is a heterogeneous mixture of sulfated glycosaminoglycans with varying chain lengths. UFH has several disadvantages, including an unpredictable anticoagulant response in individual patients, the need

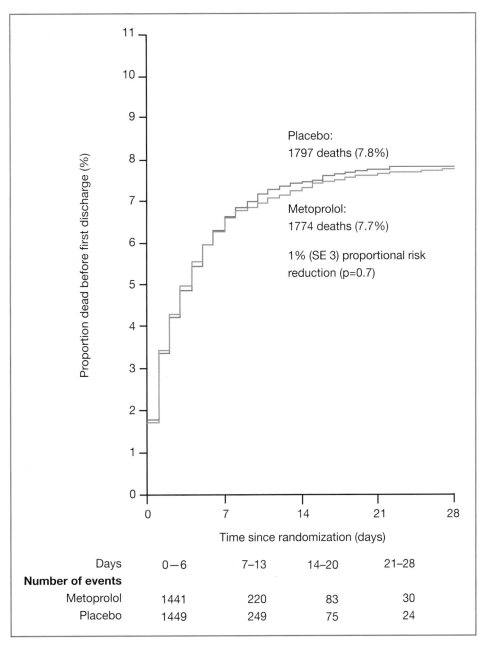

Figure 17. Effects of metoprolol allocation on death before first discharge from hospital in the COMMITT CCS2 Trial. Reproduced from Chen ZM, Pan HC, Chen YP, Peto R, Collins R, Jiang LX, Xie JX, Liu LS. Early intravenous then oral metoprolol in 45 852 patients with acute myocardial infarction: randomised placebo-controlled trial. *Lancet.* 2005;366:1622-1632,[185] with permission from Elsevier.

for IV administration, and the requirement for frequent monitoring of the activated partial thromboplastin time (aPTT). Heparin can also stimulate platelet activation, causing thrombocytopenia.

When UFH is used as adjunctive therapy with fibrin-specific lytics in STEMI, the current recommendations call for a bolus dose of 60 units/kg followed by infusion at a rate of 12 units/kg per hour (a maximum bolus of 4000 units and infusion of 1000 units/h for patients weighing >70 kg). An aPTT of 50 to 70 seconds is considered optimal.

The duration of therapy is 48 hours. The available data do not suggest a benefit from prolonging an infusion of heparin beyond this time in the absence of continuing indications for anticoagulation.

Low-Molecular-Weight Heparin

Low-molecular-weight heparins (LMWHs) have been found to be superior to UFH in patients with STEMI in terms of overall grade of flow (Thrombolysis in Myocardial Infarction [TIMI] grade)[186,187] and reducing the frequency of ischemic complications,[188] with a trend to a 14% reduction in mortality rates in a meta-analysis.[189] No superiority was found in studies in which an invasive strategy (PCI) was used.

Two randomized, controlled trials have compared UFH with LMWH as ancillary treatment to fibrinolysis in the out-of-hospital setting.[158,190] Administration of LMWH for patients with STEMI showed superiority in composite end points compared with UFH. But this benefit must be balanced against the *increase in intracranial hemorrhage in patients >75 years of age* who received LMWH (enoxaparin).[158]

LMWH is an acceptable alternative to UFH in the ED as ancillary therapy for patients <75 years of age who are receiving fibrinolytic therapy, provided that significant renal dysfunction (CrCl <30 mL/min) is not present. UFH is recommended for patients ≥75 years of age as ancillary therapy to fibrinolysis and for any STEMI patient who is undergoing revascularization.

In patients with STEMI who are not receiving fibrinolysis or revascularization, LMWH (specifically enoxaparin) may be considered an acceptable alternative to UFH in the ED setting. Dosing of enoxaparin for STEMI patients is based on age, weight, and renal function. An initial 30 mg IV bolus dose is recommended only for patients <75 years of age. If used, the bolus dose is given 15 minutes before the maintenance dose. Patients <75 years of age should then receive enoxaparin 1 mg/kg subcutaneously every 12 hours (maximum 100 mg per dose for the first 2 doses only). For patients ≥75 years of age, reduce the dose to 0.75 mg/kg every 12 hours (maximum 75 mg per dose for the first 2 doses). In patients with CrCl <30 mL/min, the dose should

be 1 mg/kg subcutaneously every 24 hours. Therapy should be maintained for the duration of hospitalization, up to 8 days.

The use of heparin in ACS and as an adjunct to other treatments can increase major bleeding and cause mortality. Healthcare providers administering heparin should be familiar with its use in different ACS settings and strategies. Preferably the administration of heparin and other therapies should be protocol driven. The *ECC Handbook* can serve as a general reference. The updated ACC/AHA Focused Guideline Recommendations for STEMI are presented in the FYI. Providers need to be aware of recent trials and new guidelines and recommendations as they emerge.

ADP Antagonists (Thienopyridines) in STEMI

Clopidogrel

Clopidogrel irreversibly inhibits the platelet adenosine diphosphate receptor, resulting in a reduction in platelet aggregation through a different mechanism than aspirin. Since the publication of *ECC Guidelines 2005,* several important clopidogrel studies have been published and reviewed by the ACC/AHA STEMI writing group that document its efficacy for patients with STEMI. Clopidogrel was approved by the FDA for use in patients with STEMI, either with or without fibrinolytic therapy, in 2006. Approval was based on results of the Clopidogrel as Adjunctive Reperfusion Therapy (CLARITY-TIMI 28) and COMMIT CCS-2 trials, which demonstrated increased efficacy of dual therapy with aspirin with no increase in intracerebral hemorrhage.

In patients up to 75 years of age with STEMI who are treated with fibrinolysis, aspirin, and heparin (LMWH or UFH), a 300 mg oral loading dose of clopidogrel given at the time of initial management (followed by a 75 mg daily dose for up to 8 days in hospital) improved coronary artery patency and reduced major adverse coronary events (MACE).[191] The COMMIT trial,[192] which included more than 45 000 patients, found that those receiving clopidogrel 75 mg had a highly significant 9% reduction in death, reinfarction, or stroke, corresponding to 9 fewer events per 1000 patients treated for only about 2 weeks. There was also no increase in intracerebral hemorrhage. Based on these findings, providers should administer a 300 mg oral dose of clopidogrel to ED patients up to 75 years of age with STEMI who receive aspirin, heparin, and fibrinolysis. If a PCI strategy is planned, providers should rely on protocol recommendations or instructions from an interventional cardiologist. On the basis of the CLARITY-TIMI 28 trial it appears that the administration of clopidogrel at the time of initial fibrinolytic therapy is beneficial when PCI is subsequently performed.[22A] Clopidogrel should not be administered to patients in shock and those who may require urgent surgical procedures.

ACC/AHA 2009 STEMI Focused Update: Recommendations for the Use of Thienopyridines

2009 STEMI-PCI Focused Update Recommendation

Class I

1. A loading dose of thienopyridine is recommended for STEMI patients for whom PCI is planned. Regimens should be 1 of the following:

   a. At least 300 to 600 mg of clopidogrel[†] should be given as early as possible before or at the time of primary or nonprimary PCI. *(Level of Evidence: C)*

   b. Prasugrel 60 mg should be given as soon as possible for primary PCI.[193,194] *(Level of Evidence: B)*

   c. For STEMI patients undergoing nonprimary PCI, the following regimens are recommended:

      (i) If the patient has received fibrinolytic therapy and has been given clopidogrel, clopidogrel should be continued as the thienopyridine of choice *(Level of Evidence: C)*;

      (ii) If the patient has received fibrinolytic therapy without a thienopyridine, a loading dose of 300 to 600 mg[‡] of clopidogrel should be given as the thienopyridine of choice *(Level of Evidence: C)*;

      (iii) If the patient did not receive fibrinolytic therapy, either a loading dose of 300 to 600 mg of clopidogrel should be given or, once the coronary anatomy is known and PCI is planned, a loading dose of 60 mg of prasugrel should be given promptly and no later than 1 hour after the PCI.[193,194] *(Level of Evidence: B)*

2. The duration of thienopyridine therapy should be as follows:

   a. In patients receiving a stent (BMS or drug-eluting stent [DES]) during PCI for ACS, clopidogrel 75 mg daily[194-196†] *(Level of Evidence: B)* or prasugrel 10 mg daily[194§] *(Level of Evidence: B)* should be given for at least 12 months;

   b. If the risk of morbidity because of bleeding outweighs the anticipated benefit afforded by thienopyridine therapy, earlier discontinuation should be considered. *(Level of Evidence: C)*

3. In patients taking a thienopyridine in whom CABG is planned and can be delayed, it is recommended that the drug be discontinued to allow for dissipation of the antiplatelet effect. *(Level of Evidence: C)* The period of withdrawal should be at least 5 days in patients receiving clopidogrel[197,198] *(Level of Evidence: B)* and at least 7 days in patients receiving prasugrel[194†] *(Level of Evidence: C)*, unless the need for revascularization and/or the net benefit of the thienopyridine outweighs the potential risks of excess bleeding.[199] *(Level of Evidence: C)*

Class IIb

1. Continuation of clopidogrel or prasugrel[§] beyond 15 months may be considered in patients undergoing DES placement.[194] *(Level of Evidence: C)*

Class III

1. In STEMI patients with a prior history of stroke and transient ischemic attack for whom primary PCI is planned, prasugrel is not recommended as part of a dual antiplatelet therapy regimen. *(Level of Evidence: C)*

†The optimum loading dose of clopidogrel has not been established. Randomized trials establishing its efficacy and providing data on bleeding risks used a loading dose of 300 mg orally followed by a daily oral dose of 75 mg.[193,194] Higher oral loading doses such as 600 mg or more than 900 mg[200] of clopidogrel more rapidly inhibit platelet aggregation and achieve a higher absolute level of inhibition of platelet aggregation, but the additive clinical efficacy and safety of higher oral loading doses have not been rigorously established. The necessity for giving a loading dose of clopidogrel before PCI is driven by the pharmacokinetics of clopidogrel, for which several hours are required to achieve desired levels of platelet inhibition. For post-PCI patients receiving a stent (BMS or DES), a daily maintenance dose should be given for at least 12 months and for up to 15 months unless the risk of bleeding outweighs the anticipated net benefit afforded by a thienopyridine.

‡Clopidogrel loading dose after fibrinolytic therapy: For patients given fibrin- and non–fibrin-specific fibrinolytic drugs who are undergoing PCI within 24 hours, 300 mg; for patients given a fibrin-specific fibrinolytic undergoing PCI after more than 24 hours, 300 to 600 mg; for patients given a non–fibrin-specific fibrinolytic undergoing PCI between 24 and 48 hours, 300 mg; for patients given a non–fibrin-specific fibrinolytic undergoing PCI after 48 hours, 300 to 600 mg.

§Patients weighing <60 kg have an increased exposure to the active metabolite of prasugrel and an increased risk of bleeding on a 10-mg once-daily maintenance dose. Consideration should be given to lowering the maintenance dose to 5 mg in patients who weigh <60 kg. The effectiveness and safety of the 5-mg dose have not been studied prospectively. For post-PCI patients receiving a stent (BMS or DES), a daily maintenance dose should be given for at least 12 months and for up to 15 months unless the risk of bleeding outweighs the anticipated net benefit afforded by a thienopyridine. Do not use prasugrel in patients with active pathological bleeding or a history of transient ischemic attack or stroke. In patients ≥75 years of age, prasugrel is generally not recommended because of the increased risk of fatal and intracranial bleeding and uncertain benefit, except in high-risk situations (patients with diabetes or a history of prior MI) in which its effect appears to be greater and its use may be considered. Do not start prasugrel in patients likely to undergo urgent CABG. When possible, discontinue prasugrel at least 7 days before any surgery. Additional risk factors for bleeding include body weight <60 kg, propensity to bleed, and concomitant use of medications that increase the risk of bleeding (eg, warfarin, heparin, fibrinolytic therapy, or chronic use of nonsteroidal anti-inflammatory drugs).

Critical Concept

Prehospital Administration of ADP Antagonists

Providers should refrain from administration of clopidogrel or prasugrel out of hospital unless and until a treatment strategy and reperfusion status have been determined by an experienced physician, planned protocol, or PCI team.

- Patients requiring urgent surgical intervention for complications of MI and left main or 3 vessel disease in shock should not receive clopidogrel or prasugrel.
- Patients 75 years of age and older should not receive a loading dose of clopidogrel or prasugrel.

Prasugrel

Prasugrel, another ADP antagonist, has been found to have greater inhibition of platelet aggregation and faster onset of action than clopidogrel. The TRITON-TIMI 38 trial examined the effects of prasugrel and clopidogrel in patients with moderate- to high-risk ACS, including more than 3500 patients with STEMI.[194] The trial showed that, relative to clopidogrel, prasugrel decreased the incidence of major adverse cardiac events (primarily due to lower rates of non-fatal MI) but was associated with an increase in TIMI major bleeding. The study favored the use of prasugrel when the combined endpoint of all-cause mortality, ischemic events, and major bleeding was examined ("net clinical benefit").

A post hoc analysis of the TRITON-TIMI 38 trial revealed 3 subgroups of patients who did not have a favorable net clinical benefit or had net harm. The use of prasugrel in patients with history of stroke or transient ischemic attack (TIA) before enrollment had net harm from prasugrel treatment. Patients weighing less than 60 kg and those who were 75 years of age and older did not have net benefit from prasugrel therapy. As a result of this analysis, the use of prasugrel is contraindicated in patients with prior TIA or stroke. A dose reduction is recommended in patients <60 kg. The risk-benefit ratio should be considered before use of prasugrel in patients 75 years of age and older.

Prasugrel (60 mg loading dose followed by maintenance dose of 5 or 10 mg daily, depending on patient weight) may be substituted for clopidogrel after angiography in patients with STEMI who are not at high risk for bleeding. It is not recommended for patients managed with fibrinolysis. There are no data to support the use of prasugrel in the ED or prehospital setting.

ACE Inhibitor Therapy

In general, ACE inhibitor therapy will not be initiated by providers in the ED. ACE inhibitor therapy is usually started in hospital after reperfusion therapy has been accomplished and the patient is hemodynamically stable. Administration of an oral ACE inhibitor is recommended within the first 24 hours after onset of symptoms in STEMI patients with pulmonary congestion or LV ejection fraction <40% in the absence of hypotension (SBP <100 mm Hg or less than 30 mm Hg below baseline). Additional indications include patients with hypertension, chronic kidney disease, or diabetes. Oral ACE inhibitor therapy should be considered for all other patients with AMI with or without early reperfusion therapy.

IV ACE inhibitor therapy is contraindicated within the first 24 hours of AMI and should not be used for control of hypertension early in the management of AMI patients.

HMG Coenzyme A Reductase Inhibitors (Statins)

A variety of studies document consistent reduction in incidence of MACE (eg, reinfarction, recurrent angina, rehospitalization, stroke) when statin treatment is administered within a few days after onset of an ACS.[201-204] There is little data to suggest that this therapy should be initiated in the ED; but early initiation of statin therapy (within 24 hours of presentation) is safe and feasible in patients with an ACS or AMI. If patients are already on statin therapy, it should be continued.

Therapy for Cardiac Arrhythmias

Treatment of ventricular arrhythmias during and after AMI has been a controversial topic for 2 decades. Primary VF accounts for the majority of early deaths during AMI. The incidence of primary VF is highest during the first 4 hours after onset of symptoms but remains an important contributor to mortality during the first 24 hours. Secondary VF occurring in the setting of congestive heart failure or cardiogenic shock can also contribute to death from AMI. VF is a less common cause of death in the hospital with the early use of fibrinolytics in conjunction with β-blockers.

Although prophylaxis with lidocaine reduces the incidence of VF, an analysis of data from ISIS-3 and a meta-analysis suggest that lidocaine increased all-cause mortality rates.[205] For this reason the practice of prophylactic administration of lidocaine has been abandoned. Routine administration of magnesium to patients with MI has no significant clinical mortality benefit, particularly in patients receiving fibrinolytic therapy. The definitive study on the subject is ISIS-4.[154]

Electrocardiography

"The 12-lead ECG is central to the triage of patients with chest discomfort. A 12-lead ECG should be performed and shown to an experienced emergency physician within 10 minutes of ED arrival on all patients with chest discomfort."

The 12-lead ECG is central to the triage of patients with chest discomfort. A 12-lead ECG should be performed and shown to an emergency physician within 10 minutes of ED arrival of all patients with chest discomfort. The 12-lead ECG is imprecise but can be used to initially classify patients into groups that trigger further diagnostic testing and therapeutic strategies. Three groups can initially be defined: patients with ST-segment elevation, patients with ST-segment depression and/or dynamic T-wave inversion, and patients with nondiagnostic or normal ECGs (Figure 18).

In the Gusto IIB Trial Electrocardiographic substudy, ST-segment elevation predicted acute MI on presentation in 89% of patients.[206] In addition, ST-segment deviation and T-wave inversion were prognostic for acute MI on presentation, death, and reinfarction in hospital (Table 3).

The 12-lead ECG is used to initially sort patients into 1 of 3 categories based on the presence or absence of ST-segment deviation and new or presumably new left bundle branch block (LBBB). Patients with ST-segment elevation or new LBBB (Figure 18A) are evaluated for rapid reperfusion. Those with high-risk NSTEMI and an ACS (Figure 18B) are treated with aggressive antiplatelet and antithrombin therapy. Patients with a low probability of ACS events (Figure 18C) receive aspirin and undergo further risk stratification. PCI indicates percutaneous coronary intervention.

1. **STEMI:** STEMI is characterized by ST-segment elevation in 2 or more contiguous leads or new LBBB. Threshold values for ST-segement elevation consistent with STEMI are J-point elevation of 2 mm (0.2 mV) in leads V_2 and V_3* and 1 mm in all other leads or new or presumed new LBBB.

2. **High-risk unstable angina/non–ST-elevation myocardial infarction (NSTEMI):** This classification is characterized by ischemic ST-segment depression ≥0.5 mm (0.05 mV) or dynamic T-wave inversion with pain or discomfort. Nonpersistent or transient ST-segment elevation ≥0.5 mm for <20 minutes is included in this category.

3. **Intermediate or low-risk unstable angina:** Normal or nondiagnostic changes in ST segment or T waves (Box 13) are inconclusive and require further risk stratification. This classification includes patients with normal ECGs and those with ST-segment deviation of <0.5 mm (0.05 mV) or T-wave inversion of ≤0.2 mV. Serial cardiac studies (and functional testing) are appropriate.

Figure 18 shows characteristic ECG findings for the acute coronary syndromes.

*2.5 mm in men <40 year old; 1.5 mm in all women.

Table 3. Confirmation of acute MI on presentation, death, and re-infarction based on ST-segment and T-wave abnormalities.[206]

	ST Elevation and Depression	ST Elevation Only	ST Depression Only	Isolated T-wave Inversion
Patients	15%	28%	35%	22%
AMI on Enrollment	89%	81%	47%	31%
Death	6.6%	5.1%	5.0%	1.7%
Re-infarction	7.1%	5.0%	6.7%	4.2%

How to Measure ST-Segment Deviation

ST-segment deviation (either elevation or depression) must be measured precisely and uniformly (Figure 19):

1. Draw the baseline ("zero ST deviation") from the *end* of the T wave to the *beginning* of the P wave (the TP segment).

   - The conventional baseline for measuring ST deviation has been the PR segment.

- A baseline drawn from the end of the T wave to the beginning of the P wave is considered to be *a more accurate baseline* for evaluation of ST deviation than the PR segment. The TP baseline is particularly helpful in ECGs with "coved" or "concave" ST segments or hyperacute T waves.

- If the TP segment cannot be identified because of a rapid heart rate or artifact, use the PR *junction* as the baseline reference point. The PR junction is the intersection of the PR segment with the QRS complex.

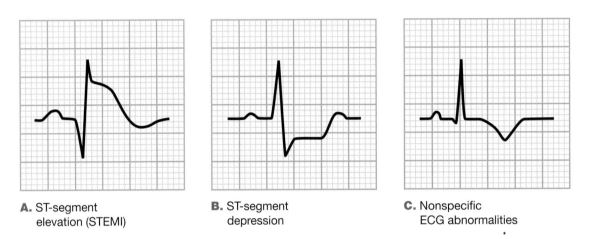

A. ST-segment elevation (STEMI)

B. ST-segment depression

C. Nonspecific ECG abnormalities

Figure 18. ECG findings of the spectrum of acute coronary syndromes. **A,** This tracing shows >1 mm ST-segment elevation, measured 0.04 seconds after the J point (STEMI). **B,** This tracing shows >0.5 mm ST-segment depression, measured 0.04 seconds after the J point. **C,** The nonspecific ST-segment and T-wave changes on this tracing are consistent with either NSTEMI or unstable angina. Cardiac markers could be positive in any of these ECG tracings.

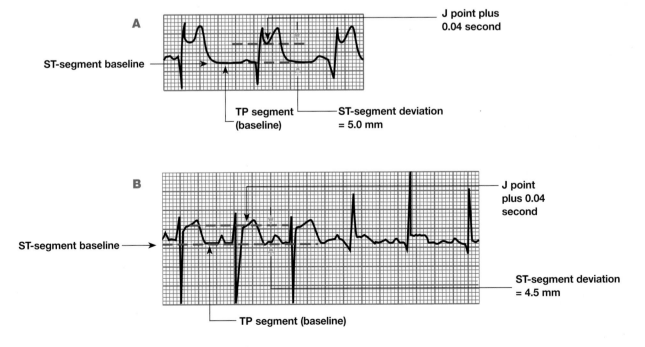

Figure 19. ECG findings of STEMI showing >1 mm ST-segment elevation, measured 0.04 second after the J point. **A,** Inferior myocardial infarction. ST segment has no low point (it is coved or concave). **B,** Anterior myocardial infarction.

2. Locate the J point, the position of juncture (angle change) between the QRS complex and the ST segment.
3. Locate 0.04 second (1 mm) after the J point. Measure the vertical deviation from this point (1 mm after the J point) either up or down to the baseline. This distance is the amount of ST deviation.

The 12-Lead ECG and Patient Triage

If STEMI is present, the patient is immediately assessed for reperfusion therapy (fibrinolytic therapy or primary PCI). Patients with ST-segment depression do not receive fibrinolytics (except true posterior MI); these agents may increase mortality and morbidity despite the magnitude and extent of ST-segment depression. Instead, antiplatelet and antithrombin therapy is indicated for these patients. Nonspecific or normal ECGs compose the largest group,

and only a minority of patients has an ACS. Serial studies and risk stratification are appropriate if coronary artery disease is thought to be an intermediate or high probability. Aspirin is indicated if no contraindications are present.

Older terminology labeled MIs as "Q wave" or "non–Q wave." These terms are electrocardiographic terms with implied pathology and are not helpful at the "front door" of the ED for risk stratification. Q waves generally are a late finding, and cardiac markers are necessary to distinguish unstable angina from MI.

Other Causes of ST-Segment Elevation

Evaluation of the patient with acute chest discomfort includes a short list of emergency differential diagnoses and a long list of other non–life-threatening causes. Initial triage involves a determination of the likelihood of these

Table 4. Conditions Other Than STEMI That Can Cause Elevation of the ST Segment of the 12-Lead ECG

Condition	Features
Normal Variant (so called male pattern)	• Seen in approximately 90% of healthy young men; therefore, normal • Elevation of 1 to 3 mm • Most marked in V_2 • Concave ST-segment
Early repolarization	• Most marked in V_4, with notching at J point • Tall, upright T waves • Reciprocal ST depression in aVR, not in aVL, when limb leads are involved
ST elevation of normal variant	• Seen in V_3 through V_5 with inverted T waves • Short QT, high QRS voltage
Left ventricular hypertrophy	• Concave • Other features of left ventricular hypertrophy
Left bundle branch block	• Concave • ST-segment deviation discordant from the QRS
Acute pericarditis	• Diffuse ST-segment elevation • Reciprocal ST-segment depression in aVR, not in aVL • Elevation seldom >5 mm • PR-segment depression
Hyperkalemia	Other features of hyperkalemia present: • Widened QRS and tall, peaked, tented T waves • Low-amplitude or absent P waves • ST segment usually downsloping
Brugada syndrome	• rSR in V_1 and V_2 • ST-segment elevation in V_1 and V_2, typically downsloping
Pulmonary embolism	• Changes simulating myocardial infarction seen often in both inferior and anteroseptal leads
Cardioversion	• Striking ST-segment elevation, often >10 mm, but lasting only a minute or two immediately after direct-current shock
Prinzmetal's angina	• Same as ST-segment elevation in infarction but transient
Acute myocardial infarction	• ST segment with a plateau or shoulder or upsloping • Reciprocal behavior between aVL and III

Adapted with permission from Wang K, Asinger RW, Marriott HJ. ST-segment elevation in conditions other than acute myocardial infarction. *N Engl J Med.* 2003;349:2128-2135.[208] © 2003 Massachusetts Medical Society.

causes. It may not be possible to rule out some of these causes, and the risk-benefit assessment involves estimating which additional causes are unlikely. This process requires integration of clinical and ECG data because time is crucial in early reperfusion. In general, reperfusion is not delayed to obtain diagnostic tests for these other conditions. Exceptions and reasonable delays in door-to-drug/balloon time include a chest x-ray or imaging study for suspected aortic dissection or an echocardiogram for suspected pericarditis. Other conditions listed in Table 4 may cause or be associated with ST-segment elevation on the initial ECG and can be difficult to discriminate from acute injury. Healthcare providers must be aware that conditions other than acute ischemic injury can cause ST-segment elevation.[207,208]

Evolution of the 12-Lead ECG in ACS

The ECG changes and "evolves" during a process that initially involves ischemia, then injury, and finally necrosis of cardiac muscle cells. Not all phases may be present in every patient, and the findings vary on the basis of patient characteristics (eg, coronary anatomy), ECG sensitivity, and location of the infarct. Early in STEMI, T waves may be tented or "peaked"; these changes are referred to as hyperacute changes. Other ECGs may show changes that are nonspecific or nondiagnostic. Finally, Q waves generally represent necrosis and are a late finding, although they may be observed early in STEMI and may decrease or resolve contrary to the usual evolutionary pattern (Figure 20).

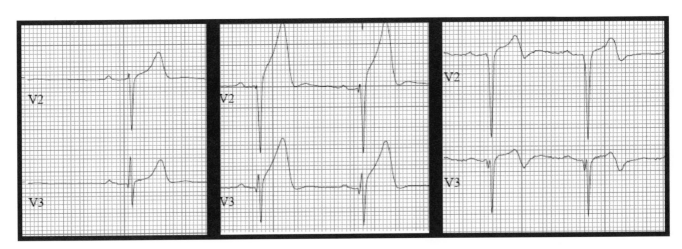

Figure 20. This figure from left to right demonstrates the ST-segment changes of STEMI. The left panel shows minimal ST-segment elevation that is concave down, possibly due to early repolarization in the baseline tracing. This patient however was having symptoms of ischemic chest discomfort and the ECG was repeated 10 minutes later. Clearly seen in the middle panel are tented and peaked ST segments. In the right panel, evolution of the ST segment and T-wave changes are seen in a tracing obtained 1 hour later immediately after PCI. The ST segments are elevated but returning to normal and the T waves are biphasic. In addition, there is a QS complex in lead V_2 and further loss of R wave in V_3. Although Q waves are generally a later finding in STEMI evolution they may occur early in approximately 50% of patients.

Instructions for Independent Study

This material is designed for you to study and learn at your own pace. There is no fee for continuing education credit for this material.

- Review the learning objectives.
- Read the text.
- Take the online test and evaluation.
- Print the completion and CE certificates.

There are ten annotated 12-lead ECGs provided for self study.

The test, evaluation, and certificates can be accessed at **www.OnlineAHA.org/STEMI**.

If you have never registered on this site, you will need to register before accessing the test, evaluation, and certificate.

ECG 1: Normal ECG

I aVR V1 V4

II aVL V2 V5

III aVF V3 V6

V1

Discussion

ECG and Anatomy of the Coronary Arteries

This diagram demonstrates very general and simplified correlations between ECG leads, the heart, and coronary anatomy. The left anterior descending (LAD) coronary artery supplies the anterior wall of the heart and a portion of the anterolateral wall of the left ventricle (LV). The right coronary artery (RCA) supplies the right ventricle and the inferior, posterior, and posterolateral wall of the LV in the majority of patients. The circumflex (Cx) coronary artery supplies the lateral wall of the heart.

The areas of myocardium supplied can be varied among patients, especially in border zones between two regions and when collateral circulation exists. At a screening level, the task of reading an ECG is *not* to localize an infarct but to recognize when regional ST-segment elevation exists consistent with an ST-elevation myocardial infarction (STEMI) caused by an occlusion of a major coronary artery.

Remember, the leads depicted sample a three-dimensional heart. Leads II, III and aVF are depicting the inferior or back wall of the heart. An occlusion of one coronary artery can affect several leads. An occlusion of the LAD at its origin involves the septum, anterior wall, lateral wall, and apex of the heart (V_1 through V_6 and I and aVL).

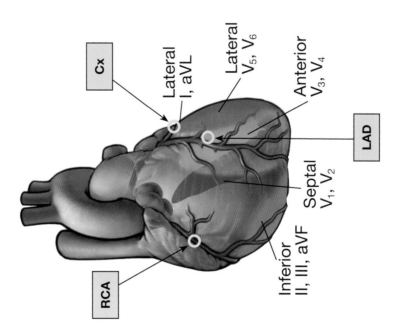

I lateral	aVR	V_1 septal	V_4 anterior
II inferior	aVL lateral	V_2 septal	V_5 lateral
III inferior	aVF inferior	V_3 anterior	V_6 lateral

ECG 2: Acute Anterior (Hyperacute) STEMI

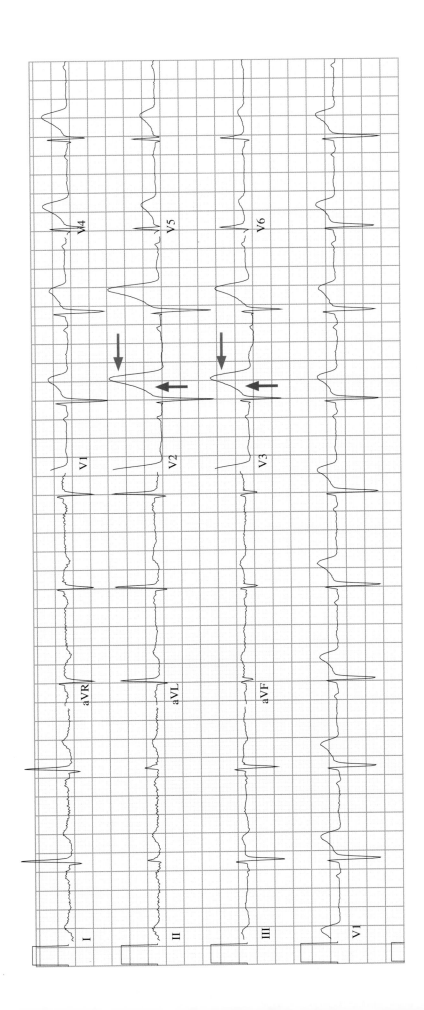

Discussion

ECG

This ECG shows early changes consistent with an acute anterior myocardial infarction. There is elevation of the ST segment (blue arrows), and very early after occlusion both the ST-segment and T-wave "point to" the area of infarction with peaking of the T-waves (red arrows), sometimes called "hyperacute change." In this ECG, notice that there is no "reciprocal" ST-segment depression.

Anatomy

This ECG pattern is due to a proximal occlusion of the LAD (yellow circle). The LAD supplies the anterior wall and septum of the left ventricle. Depending on its size and branches (diagonal branches to lateral wall) leads V_1 through V_6 and leads I and aVL may be involved. After PCI the artery is patent.

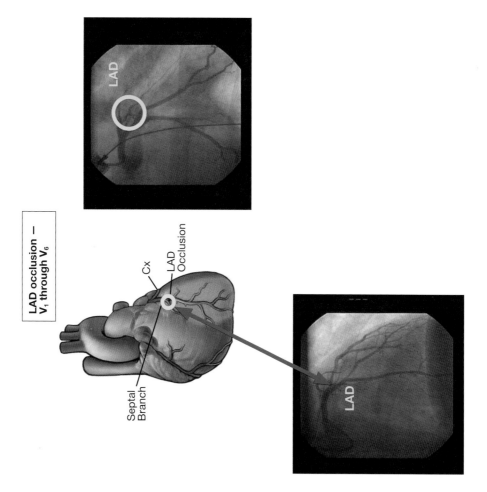

LAD occlusion —
V_1 through V_6

Cx

LAD
Occlusion

Septal
Branch

LAD

LAD

ECG 3: Acute Anterior STEMI

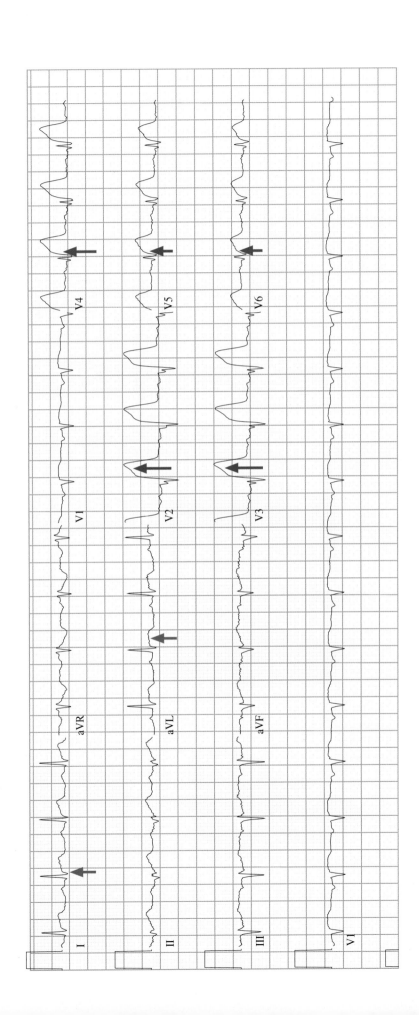

Discussion

ECG

This ECG is from a different patient, who also has a proximal LAD occlusion. It shows a later evolution of changes (A to B) with the development of extensive anterior wall and lateral wall ST-segment elevation more typical of an "injury" current. Note, however, that the T-wave is still "pointing to" the area of infarction (blue arrows). There is also now a subtle but definite infarction of the septum (septal branches of LAD), anterior wall, and anterolateral wall (diagonal branches of LAD) evidenced by small Q-waves and loss of R-wave.

Anatomy

As in ECG 2, this ECG pattern is the result of a proximal occlusion of the LAD (yellow circle). The LAD supplies the anterior wall and septum of the left ventricle. Depending on its size and branches (diagonal branches to lateral wall) leads V_1 through V_6 and leads I and aVL may be involved. Note here there is lateral wall involvement with ST-segment elevation in leads V_5, V_6, I, and aVL. Also note that even with these extensive changes there is still no reciprocal ST depression. While helpful, reciprocal ST-segment depression may not be present in all patients.

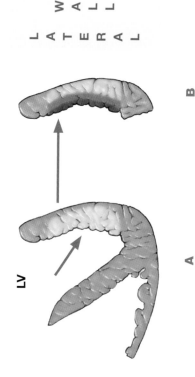

LV

LATERAL WALL

A   B

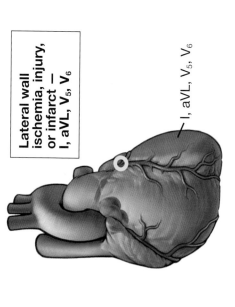

Lateral wall ischemia, injury, or infarct — I, aVL, V_5, V_6

I, aVL, V_5, V_6

ECG 4: Acute or Recent Anterior STEMI (Q-Wave)

Discussion

ECG

As the ECG evolves, the ST segment elevation (black arrows) return to baseline and the T waves become biphasic and eventually inverted.

In the anterior leads the initial positive R-wave (insert, red arrow) is lost due to myocardial necrosis of the anterior wall and the development of a "QS" complex as a sign of myocardial infarction. Traditionally, Q waves (QS complexes) were thought to occur as a late event but have been found early in many patients. This fact is important because Q waves occurring in the presence of ST-segment elevation (blue arrows) cannot definitely establish the time of the infarct and does not preclude reperfusion. Clinically the time of onset of continuous, persistent chest discomfort is most important.

Anatomy

As depicted in the evolving infarct example (A → B) the infarct has extended from endocardium to epicardium and is now transmural (100% necrosis). Here the ECG develops Q waves—a sign of infarction.

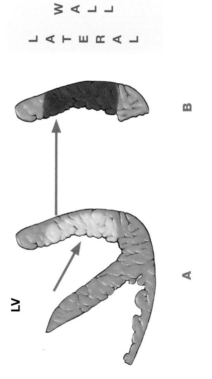

LV

A

B

LATERAL WALL

51

ECG 5: Acute Inferior STEMI

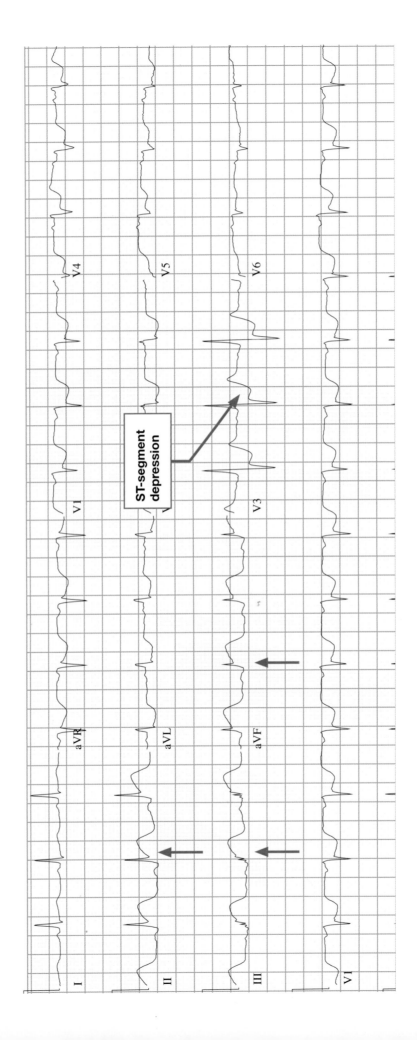

ST-segment depression

Discussion

ECG

This ECG shows a classic inferior ST-segment elevation MI with ST-segment elevation in leads II, III, and aVF (red arrows). Notice there is ST-segment depression in leads I and aVL and leads V_1 through V_4.

Anatomy

This ECG pattern is due to a proximal occlusion of the right coronary artery (blue arrows). The RCA supplies the right ventricle and inferior and posterior wall of the heart in a right coronary dominant circulation, which is seen in about 85% of people.

RCA occlusion —
II, III, aVF

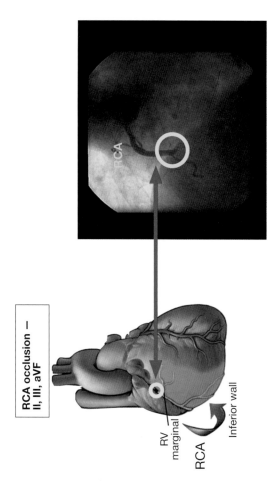

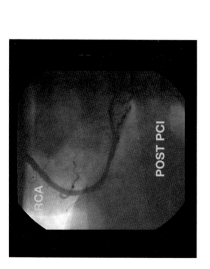

ECG 6: Acute Inferolateral

Discussion

ECG

This ECG shows a large inferior ST-segment elevation MI in leads II, III, and aVF (blue arrows). Notice that there is ST-segment depression in leads I and aVL (red arrows). This is due to reciprocal changes in the leads opposite the area of infarction. Notice also the ST-segment elevation in lateral leads V_4 through V_6 (black arrows). This is due to lateral wall involvement in an inferior MI.

Anatomy

This ECG pattern is due to a proximal occlusion of the right coronary artery. The RCA supplies the right ventricle and inferior and posterior wall of the heart in a right coronary dominant circulation, which is seen in about 85% of people. A portion of the lateral wall of the LV can be supplied by a posterolateral branch of the RCA or by a marginal branch of the Cx or a combination of both (red circle; green arrow). The lateral wall changes in the leads here are caused by an inferior wall MI as indicated by ST-segment elevations in leads II, III, and aVF.

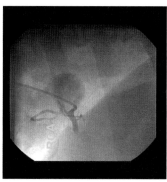

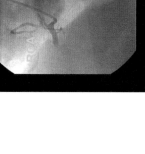

RCA

Cx

Posterior View

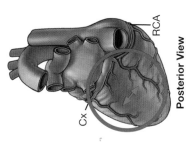

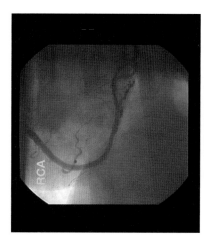

RCA

Post PCI RCA Patient

ECG 7: Inferior STEMI With RVMI

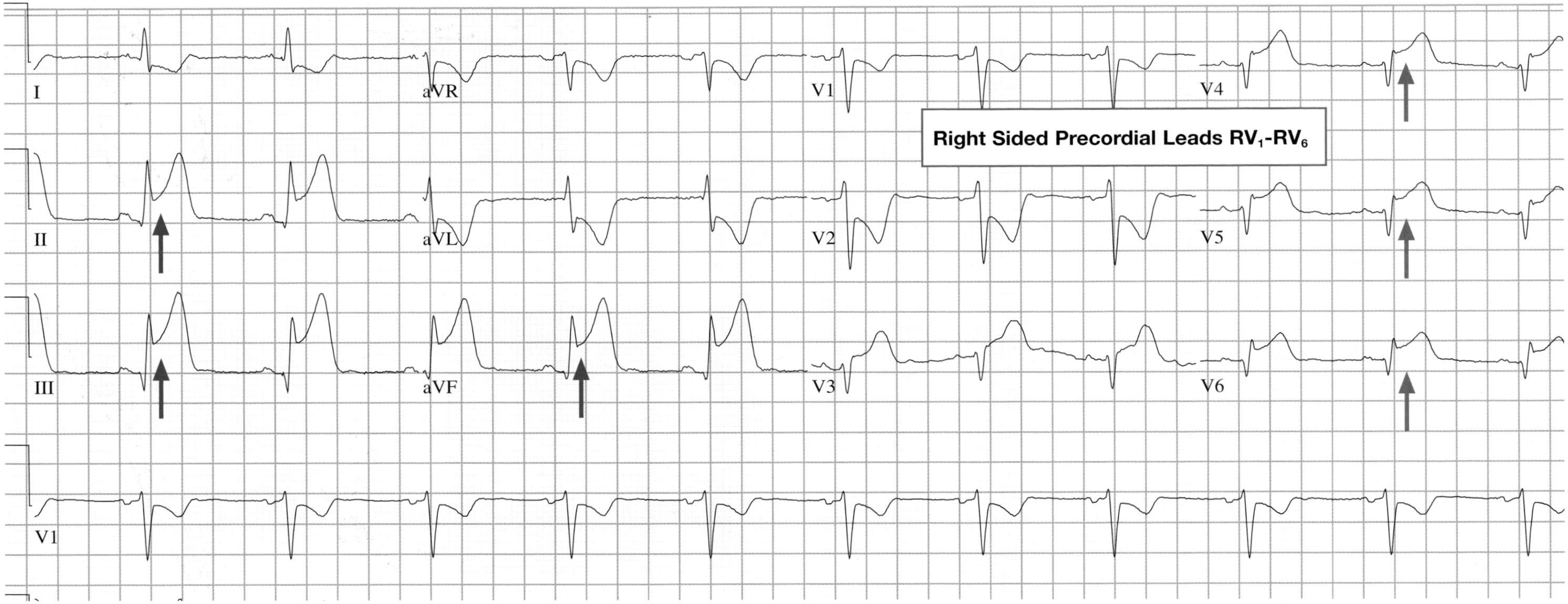

Right Sided Precordial Leads RV₁-RV₆

I

II

III

V1

aVR

aVL

aVF

V1

V2

V3

V4

V5

V6

Discussion

ECG

This ECG shows another inferior ST-segment elevation MI with ST-segment elevation in leads II, III, and aVF (blue arrows). Notice again that there is ST-segment depression in leads I and aVL. This is due to reciprocal changes in the leads opposite the area of infarction. Leads V_4 through V_6 are right precordial leads, and there is ST-segment elevation indicating an occlusion of the RV marginal branch(es) with RV ischemia/infarction (red arrows).

Anatomy

This ECG pattern is due to a proximal occlusion of the right coronary artery (blue arrows) before the RV marginal branch(es). Patients with clinically significant RV ischemia/infarction can have hypotension and even shock as the RV fails to preload the LV.

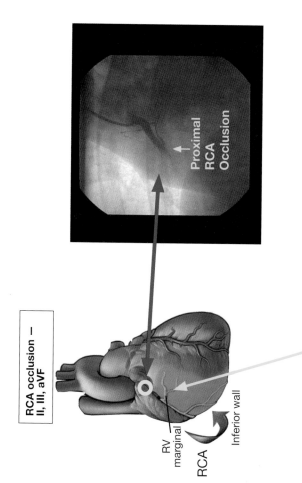

RCA occlusion — II, III, aVF

RV marginal

RCA

Inferior wall

Proximal RCA Occlusion

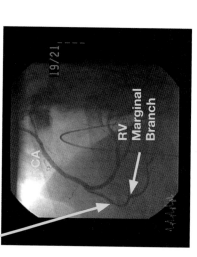

RV Marginal Branch

RCA

19/21

ECG 8: Left Bundle Branch Block

Treatment Effects Thrombolytic Therapy

Mortality based on ECG Presentation -FTT Overview

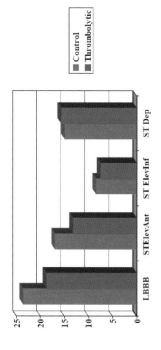

Indications for fibrinolytic therapy in suspected acute myocardial infarction: collaborative overview of early mortality and major morbidity results from all randomised trials of more than 1000 patients. Fibrinolytic Therapy Trialists' (FTT) Collaborative Group. *Lancet.* 1994;343:311-322.

The figure above shows the mortality in red for various ECG presentations in patients with MI. Note that LBBB has the highest mortality overall, approaching 25%. This is due to a large amount of myocardium involved in the MI when STEMI causes LBBB. Note that patients treated with fibrinolytic therapy had a mortality in all groups except ST-segment depression.

Discussion

ECG

This ECG shows a wide QRS complex (QRS ≥0.12 second). The QRS pattern is consistent with a block in the electrical impulse transmission to the left ventricle.

Anatomy

Normally the LV is activated by the left anterior and left posterior division of the left bundle branch of the electrical system of the heart. When left bundle branch block (LBBB) occurs, activation of the LV muscle must occur more slowly through the right bundle branch. This results in a wide QRS complex, which is due to distortion of the initial and terminal electrical vectors of the heart.

STEMI Implications

The distortion of the QRS complex makes interpretation of ST-segment shifts unreliable and obscures the diagnosis of STEMI. Hence, new or presumably new LBBB is an indication to consider reperfusion therapy when the clinical situation suggests STEMI. LBBB occurs when a large amount of myocardium is associated with an anterior MI.

ECG 9: Right Bundle Branch Block

Discussion

ECG

This ECG also shows a wide QRS complex (QRS ≥0.12 second). The QRS pattern is consistent with a block in the electrical impulse transmission to the RV. Note the rSr′ complex in precordial lead V_1.

Anatomy

The RV is activated by the right bundle branch of the electrical system of the heart. Activation of the RV muscle must now occur more slowly through the left bundle branch, which causes a wide QRS complex.

STEMI Implications

The distortion of the QRS complex makes interpretation of ST-segment shifts more difficult, but RBBB distorts only the terminal end of the QRS complex and has characteristic ST-segment and T-wave changes. Although new RBBB increases mortality with MI, it is often possible for experienced ECG readers to identify the presence of STEMI. Also, the initial vector of the QRS complex is not altered, so Q waves can be identified when present. Note ST-segment elevation in insert box leads V_2 and V_3.

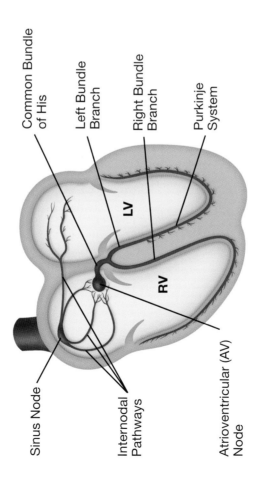

Sinus Node

Internodal Pathways

Atrioventricular (AV) Node

Common Bundle of His

Left Bundle Branch

Right Bundle Branch

Purkinje System

LV

RV

ECG 10: Early Repolarization

Discussion

ECG

This ECG is normal but demonstrates ST-segment elevation in multiple leads, an event called "early repolarization." Perhaps the most difficult distinction to make is distinguishing between ST-segment changes due to acute injury from borderline changes due to the normal ECG variant early repolarization. As you recall, the T wave is the major deflection occurring when the ventricle repolarizes and resets for the next contraction. When a portion of the heart starts this process early it can cause deviation of the ST segment from the isoelectric baseline. This is most prominent in the early precordial leads (eg, leads V_1, V_2, and V_3). The displacement of the ST segment can be as much as 1 to 2 mm.

STEMI Implications

Although not perfect, certain ECG characteristics suggest early repolarization. These include a gently upsloping and curving downward or sagging of the ST segment, producing the so-called "smiley face." Contrast this with the junctional elevation and horizontal or straight ST-segment and the curving upward of "sad face" of the STEMI examples you have seen.

1. Cannon CP, Braunwald E. Time to reperfusion: The critical modulator in thrombolysis and primary angioplasty. *J Thromb Thrombolysis*. 1996;3:117-125.

2. Rogers WJ, Bowlby LJ, Chandra NC, French WJ, Gore JM, Lambrew CT, Rubison RM, Tiefenbrunn AJ, Weaver WD. Treatment of myocardial infarction in the United States (1990 to 1993): Observations from the National Registry of Myocardial Infarction. *Circulation*. 1994;90:2103-2114.

3. Rogers WJ, Canto JG, Lambrew CT, Tiefenbrunn AJ, Kinkaid B, Shoultz DA, Frederick PD, Every N. Temporal trends in the treatment of over 1.5 million patients with myocardial infarction in the U.S. from 1990 through 1999: The National Registry of Myocardial Infarction 1, 2 and 3. *J Am Coll Cardiol*. 2000;36:2056-2063.

4. Andersen HR, Nielsen TT, Rasmussen K, Thuesen L, Kelbaek H, Thayssen P, Abildgaard U, Pedersen F, Madsen JK, Grande P, Villadsen AB, Krusell LR, Haghfelt T, Lomholt P, Husted SE, Vigholt E, Kjaergard HK, Mortensen LS. A comparison of coronary angioplasty with fibrinolytic therapy in acute myocardial infarction. *N Engl J Med*. 2003;349:733-742.

5. Brodie BR, Stuckey TD, Wall TC, Kissling G, Hansen CJ, Muncy DB, Weintraub RA, Kelly TA. Importance of time to reperfusion for 30-day and late survival and recovery of left ventricular function after primary angioplasty for acute myocardial infarction. *J Am Coll Cardiol*. 1998;32:1312-1319.

6. Cannon CP, Gibson CM, Lambrew CT, Shoultz DA, Levy D, French WJ, Gore JM, Weaver WD, Rogers WJ, Tiefenbrunn AJ. Relationship of symptom-onset-to-balloon time and door-to-balloon time with mortality in patients undergoing angioplasty for acute myocardial infarction. *JAMA*. 2000;283:2941-2947.

7. Chiriboga D, Yarzebski J, Goldberg RJ, Gore JM, Alpert JS. Temporal trends (1975 through 1990) in the incidence and case-fatality rates of primary ventricular fibrillation complicating acute myocardial infarction: a communitywide perspective. *Circulation*. 1994;89:998-1003.

8. Franzosi MG, Santoro E, De Vita C, Geraci E, Lotto A, Maggioni AP, Mauri F, Rovelli F, Santoro L, Tavazzi L, Tognoni G. Ten-year follow-up of the first megatrial testing thrombolytic therapy in patients with acute myocardial infarction: results of the Gruppo Italiano per lo Studio della Sopravvivenza nell'Infarto-1 study. The GISSI Investigators. *Circulation*. 1998;98:2659-2665.

9. Goldberg RJ, Mooradd M, Gurwitz JH, Rogers WJ, French WJ, Barron HV, Gore JM. Impact of time to treatment with tissue plasminogen activator on morbidity and mortality following acute myocardial infarction (the second national registry of myocardial infarction). *Am J Cardiol*. 1998;82:259-264.

10. GUSTO Investigators, Kleiman NS, White HD, Ohman EM, Ross AM, Woodlief LH, Califf RM, Holmes DR Jr, Bates E, Pfisterer M, Vahanian A, et al. Mortality within 24 hours of thrombolysis for myocardial infarction. The importance of early reperfusion. The GUSTO Investigators, Global Utilization of Streptokinase and Tissue Plasminogen Activator for Occluded Coronary Arteries. *Circulation*. 1994;90:2658-2665.

11. Rawles J. Halving of mortality at 1 year by domiciliary thrombolysis in the Grampian Region Early Anistreplase Trial (GREAT). *J Am Coll Cardiol*. 1994;23:1-5.

12. Rawles J. GREAT: 10 year survival of patients with suspected acute myocardial infarction in a randomised comparison of prehospital and hospital thrombolysis. *Heart*. 2003;89:563-564.

13. Cantor WJ, Goodman SG, Cannon CP, Murphy SA, Charlesworth A, Braunwauld E, Langer A. Early cardiac catheterization is associated with lower mortality only among high-risk patients with ST- and non-ST-elevation acute coronary syndromes: observations from the OPUS-TIMI 16 trial. *Am Heart J*. 2005;149:275-283.

14. Steg PG, Bonnefoy E, Chabaud S, Lapostolle F, Dubien PY, Cristofini P, Leizorovicz A, Touboul P. Impact of time to treatment on mortality after prehospital fibrinolysis or primary angioplasty: data from the CAPTIM randomized clinical trial. *Circulation*. 2003;108:2851-2856.

15. Hochman JS, Sleeper LA, Godfrey E, McKinlay SM, Sanborn T, Col J, LeJemtel T. SHould we emergently revascularize Occluded Coronaries for cardiogenic shocK: an international randomized trial of emergency PTCA/CABG-trial design. The SHOCK Trial Study Group. *Am Heart J*. 1999;137:313-321.

16. Nallamothu B, Fox KA, Kennelly BM, Van de Werf F, Gore JM, Steg PG, Granger CB, Dabbous OH, Kline-Rogers E, Eagle KA. Relationship of treatment delays and mortality in patients undergoing fibrinolysis and primary percutaneous coronary intervention. The Global Registry of Acute Coronary Events. *Heart*. 2007;93:1552-1555.

17. Fox KA, Steg PG, Eagle KA, Goodman SG, Anderson FA Jr, Granger CB, Flather MD, Budaj A, Quill A, Gore JM. Decline in rates of death and heart failure in acute coronary syndromes, 1999-2006. *JAMA*. 2007;297:1892-1900.

18. Zeymer U, Neuhaus KL, Wegscheider K, Tebbe U, Molhoek P, Schroder R. Effects of thrombolytic therapy in acute inferior myocardial infarction with or without right ventricular involvement: HIT-4 Trial Group (Hirudin for Improvement of Thrombolysis). *J Am Coll Cardiol*. 1998;32:876-881.

19. Ornato JP. The ST-segment-elevation myocardial infarction chain of survival. *Circulation*. 2007;116:6-9.

20. Luepker RV, Raczynski JM, Osganian S, Goldberg RJ, Finnegan JR Jr, Hedges JR, Goff DC Jr, Eisenberg MS, Zapka JG, Feldman HA, Labarthe DR, McGovern PG, Cornell CE, Proschan MA, Simons-Morton DG. Effect of a community intervention on patient delay and emergency medical service use in acute coronary heart disease: The Rapid Early Action for Coronary Treatment (REACT) Trial. *JAMA*. 2000;284:60-67.

21. McGinn AP, Rosamond WD, Goff DC Jr, Taylor HA, Miles JS, Chambless L. Trends in prehospital delay time and use of emergency medical services for acute myocardial infarction: experience in 4 US communities from 1987-2000. *Am Heart J*. 2005;150:392-400.

22. Kushner FG, Hand M, Smith SC Jr, King SB III, Anderson JL, Antman EM, Bailey SR, Bates ER, Blankenship JC, Casey DJ Jr, Green LA, Hochman JS, Jacobs AK, Krumholz HM, Morrison DA, Ornato JP, Pearle DL, Peterson ED, Sloan MA, Whitlow PL, Williams DO. 2009 Focused Updates: ACC/AHA Guidelines for the Management of Patients With ST-Elevation Myocardial Infarction (updating the 2004 Guideline and 2007 Focused Update) and ACC/AHA/SCAI Guidelines on Percutaneous Coronary Intervention (updating the 2005 Guideline and 2007 Focused Update): a report of the American College of Cardiology Foundation/American Heart Association Task Force on Practice Guidelines. *Circulation*. 2009;120:2271-2306.

22A. Antman EM, Hand M, Armstrong PW, Bates ER, Green LA, Halasyamani LK, Hochman JS, Krumholz HM, Lamas GA, Mullany CJ, Pearle DL, Sloan MA, Smith SC Jr, Anbe DT, Kushner FG, Ornato JP, Jacobs AK, Adams CD, Anderson JL, Buller CE, Creager MA, Ettinger SM, Halperin JL, Hunt SA, Lytle BW, Nishimura R, Page RL, Riegel B, Tarkington LG, Yancy CW. 2007 Focused Update of the ACC/AHA 2004 Guidelines for the Management of Patients With ST-Elevation Myocardial Infarction: a report of the American College of Cardiology/American Heart Association Task Force on Practice Guidelines: developed in collaboration with the Canadian Cardiovascular Society endorsed by the American Academy of Family Physicians: 2007 Writing Group to Review New Evidence and Update the ACC/AHA 2004 Guidelines for the Management of Patients With ST-Elevation Myocardial Infarction, Writing on Behalf of the 2004 Writing Committee. *Circulation*. 2008;117:296-329.

23. Antman EM, Anbe DT, Armstrong PW, Bates ER, Green LA, Hand M, Hochman JS, Krumholz HM, Kushner FG, Lamas GA, Mullany CJ, Ornato JP, Pearle DL, Sloan MA, Smith SC Jr. ACC/AHA guidelines for the management of patients with ST-elevation myocardial infarction—executive summary. A report of the American College of Cardiology/American Heart Association Task Force on Practice Guidelines (Writing Committee to revise the 1999 guidelines for the management of patients with acute myocardial infarction). *J Am Coll Cardiol*. 2004;44:671-719.

24. Armstrong PW, Collen D, Antman E. Fibrinolysis for acute myocardial infarction: the future is here and now. *Circulation*. 2003;107:2533-2537.

25. Jacobs AK, Antman EM, Faxon DP, Gregory T, Solis P. Development of systems of care for ST-elevation myocardial infarction patients: executive summary. *Circulation*. 2007;116:217-230.

26. Kereiakes DJ, Weaver WD, Anderson JL, Feldman T, Gibler B, Aufderheide T, Williams DO, Martin LH, Anderson LC, Martin JS, et al. Time delays in the diagnosis and treatment of acute myocardial infarction: a tale of eight cities. Report from the Pre-hospital Study Group and the Cincinnati Heart Project. *Am Heart J*. 1990;120:773-780.

27. Siepmann DB, Mann NC, Hedges JR, Daya MR. Association between prepayment systems and emergency medical services use among patients with acute chest discomfort syndrome. For the Rapid Early Action for Coronary Treatment (REACT) Study. *Ann Emerg Med*. 2000;35:573-578.

28. Access to timely and optimal care of patients with acute coronary syndromes: community planning considerations. A report by the National Heart Attack Alert Program. *J Thromb Thrombolysis*. 1998;6:19-46.

29. Kereiakes DJ, Gibler WB, Martin LH, Pieper KS, Anderson LC. Relative importance of emergency medical system transport and the prehospital electrocardiogram on reducing hospital time delay to therapy for acute myocardial infarction: a preliminary report from the Cincinnati Heart Project. *Am Heart J*. 1992;123(pt 1):835-840.

30. Aufderheide TP, Hendley GE, Woo J, Lawrence S, Valley V, Teichman SL. A prospective evaluation of prehospital 12-lead ECG application in chest pain patients. *J Electrocardiol*. 1992;24(suppl):8-13.

31. Brown AL, Mann NC, Daya M, Goldberg R, Meischke H, Taylor J, Smith K, Osganian S, Cooper L. Demographic, belief, and situational factors influencing the decision to utilize emergency medical services among chest pain patients. Rapid Early Action for Coronary Treatment (REACT) study. *Circulation*. 2000;102:173-178.

32. Hedges JR, Feldman HA, Bittner V, Goldberg RJ, Zapka J, Osganian SK, Murray DM, Simons-Morton DG, Linares A, Williams J, Luepker RV, Eisenberg MS. Impact of community intervention to reduce patient delay time on use of reperfusion therapy for acute myocardial infarction: rapid early action for coronary treatment (REACT) trial. REACT Study Group. *Acad Emerg Med*. 2000;7:862-872.

33. Meischke H, Dulberg EM, Schaeffer SS, Henwood DK, Larsen MP, Eisenberg MS. 'Call fast, Call 911': a direct mail campaign to reduce patient delay in acute myocardial infarction. *Am J Public Health*. 1997;87:1705-1709.

34. Meischke H, Diehr P, Rowe S, Cagle A, Eisenberg M. Evaluation of a public education program delivered by firefighters on early recognition of a heart attack. *Eval Health Prof*. 2004;27:3-21.

35. Keeley EC, Boura JA, Grines CL. Primary angioplasty versus intravenous thrombolytic therapy for acute myocardial infarction: a quantitative review of 23 randomised trials. *Lancet*. 2003;361:13-20.

36. Zijlstra F. Long-term benefit of primary angioplasty compared to thrombolytic therapy for acute myocardial infarction. *Eur Heart J*. 2000;21:1487-1489.

37. Busk M, Maeng M, Rasmussen K, Kelbaek H, Thayssen P, Abildgaard U, Vigholt E, Mortensen LS, Thuesen L, Kristensen SD, Nielsen TT, Andersen HR. The Danish multicentre randomized study of fibrinolytic therapy vs. primary angioplasty in acute myocardial infarction (the DANAMI-2 trial): outcome after 3 years follow-up. *Eur Heart J*. 2008;29:1259-1266.

38. *Directory of Cardiac Catheterization Laboratories in the U.S.* Society for Cardiac Angiography and Interventions: Bethesda, Md; 1999.

39. Blankenship JC, Haldis TA, Wood GC, Skelding KA, Scott T, Menapace FJ. Rapid triage and transport of patients with ST-elevation myocardial infarction for percutaneous coronary intervention in a rural health system. *Am J Cardiol.* 2007;100:944-948.

40. Hata N, Kobayashi N, Imaizumi T, Yokoyama S, Shinada T, Tanabe J, Shiiba K, Suzuki Y, Matsumoto H, Mashiko K. Use of an air ambulance system improves time to treatment of patients with acute myocardial infarction. *Intern Med.* 2006;45:45-50.

41. Straumann E, Yoon S, Naegeli B, Frielingsdorf J, Gerber A, Schuiki E, Bertel O. Hospital transfer for primary coronary angioplasty in high risk patients with acute myocardial infarction. *Heart.* 1999;82:415-419.

42. Sternbach G, Sumchai AP. Is aeromedical transport of patients during acute myocardial infarction safe? *J Emerg Med.* 1989;7:73-77.

43. Bellinger RL, Califf RM, Mark DB, Weber RA, Collins P, Stone J, Phillips HR 3rd, German L, Stack RS. Helicopter transport of patients during acute myocardial infarction. *Am J Cardiol.* 1988;61:718-722.

44. Nallamothu BK, Bates ER, Wang Y, Bradley EH, Krumholz HM. Driving times and distances to hospitals with percutaneous coronary intervention in the United States: implications for pre-hospital triage of patients with ST-elevation myocardial infarction. *Circulation.* 2006;113:1189-1195.

45. Le May MR, So DY, Dionne R, Glover CA, Froeschl MP, Wells GA, Davies RF, Sherrard HL, Maloney J, Marquis JF, O'Brien ER, Trickett J, Poirier P, Ryan SC, Ha A, Joseph PG, Labinaz M. A citywide protocol for primary PCI in ST-segment elevation myocardial infarction. *N Engl J Med.* 2008;358:231-240.

46. Hochman JS, Sleeper LA, Webb JG, Dzavik V, Buller CE, Aylward P, Col J, White HD. Early revascularization and long-term survival in cardiogenic shock complicating acute myocardial infarction. *JAMA.* 2006;295:2511-2515.

47. Libby P. Current concepts of the pathogenesis of the acute coronary syndromes. *Circulation.* 2001;104:365-372.

48. Libby P, Theroux P. Pathophysiology of coronary artery disease. *Circulation.* 2005;111:3481-3488.

49. Libby P. Molecular bases of the acute coronary syndromes. *Circulation.* 1995;91:2844-2850.

50. Behar S, Halabi M, Reicher-Reiss H, Zion M, Kaplinsky E, Mandelzweig L, Goldbourt U. Circadian variation and possible external triggers of onset of myocardial infarction. SPRINT Study Group. *Am J Med.* 1993;94:395-400.

51. Smith M, Little WC. Potential precipitating factors of the onset of myocardial infarction. *Am J Med Sci.* 1992;303:141-144.

52. Siscovick DS, Weiss NS, Fletcher RH, Lasky T. The incidence of primary cardiac arrest during vigorous exercise. *N Engl J Med.* 1984;311:874-877.

53. Siscovick DS, Weiss NS, Hallstrom AP, Inui TS, Peterson DR. Physical activity and primary cardiac arrest. *JAMA.* 1982;248:3113-3117.

54. D'Avanzo B, Santoro L, La Vecchia C, Maggioni A, Nobili A, Iacuitti G, Franceschi S. Physical activity and the risk of acute myocardial infarction. GISSI-EFRIM Investigators. Gruppo Italiano per lo Studio della Sopravvivenza nell'Infarto-Epidemiologia dei Fattori di Rischio dell'Infarto Miocardico. *Ann Epidemiol.* 1993;3:645-651.

55. Cannon CP, McCabe CH, Stone PH, Schactman M, Thompson B, Theroux P, Gibson RS, Feldman T, Kleiman NS, Tofler GH, Muller JE, Chaitman BR, Braunwald E. Circadian variation in the onset of unstable angina and non-Q-wave acute myocardial infarction (the TIMI III Registry and TIMI IIIB). *Am J Cardiol.* 1997;79:253-258.

56. Figueras J, Lidon RM. Early morning reduction in ischemic threshold in patients with unstable angina and significant coronary disease. *Circulation.* 1995;92:1737-1742.

57. Muller JE, Stone PH, Turi ZG, Rutherford JD, Czeisler CA, Parker C, Poole WK, Passamani E, Roberts R, Robertson T, et al. Circadian variation in the frequency of onset of acute myocardial infarction. *N Engl J Med.* 1985;313:1315-1322.

58. Willich SN, Levy D, Rocco MB, Tofler GH, Stone PH, Muller JE. Circadian variation in the incidence of sudden cardiac death in the Framingham Heart Study population. *Am J Cardiol.* 1987;60:801-806.

59. Peters RW. Circadian patterns and triggers of sudden cardiac death. *Cardiol Clin.* 1996;14:185-194.

60. Peters RW, Mitchell LB, Brooks MM, Echt DS, Barker AH, Capone R, Liebson PR, Greene HL. Circadian pattern of arrhythmic death in patients receiving encainide, flecainide or moricizine in the Cardiac Arrhythmia Suppression Trial (CAST). *J Am Coll Cardiol.* 1994;23:283-289.

61. Tofler GH, Gebara OC, Mittleman MA, Taylor P, Siegel W, Venditti FJ Jr, Rasmussen CA, Muller JE. Morning peak in ventricular tachyarrhythmias detected by time of implantable cardioverter/defibrillator therapy. The CPI Investigators. *Circulation.* 1995;92:1203-1208.

62. Krantz DS, Kop WJ, Santiago HT, Gottdiener JS. Mental stress as a trigger of myocardial ischemia and infarction. *Cardiol Clin.* 1996;14:271-287.

63. el-Tamimi H, Mansour M, Pepine CJ, Wargovich TJ, Chen H. Circadian variation in coronary tone in patients with stable angina. Protective role of the endothelium. *Circulation.* 1995;92:3201-3205.

64. Larson DM, Menssen KM, Sharkey SW, Duval S, Schwartz RS, Harris J, Meland JT, Unger BT, Henry TD. "False-positive" cardiac catheterization laboratory activation among patients with suspected ST-segment elevation myocardial infarction. *JAMA.* 2007;298:2754-2760.

65. Peberdy MA, Ornato JP. Coronary artery disease in women. *Heart Dis Stroke.* 1992;1:315-319.

66. Douglas PS, Ginsburg GS. The evaluation of chest pain in women. *N Engl J Med.* 1996;334:1311-1315.

67. Sullivan AK, Holdright DR, Wright CA, Sparrow JL, Cunningham D, Fox KM. Chest pain in women: clinical, investigative, and prognostic features. *BMJ.* 1994;308:883-886.

68. Solomon CG, Lee TH, Cook EF, Weisberg MC, Brand DA, Rouan GW, Goldman L. Comparison of clinical presentation of acute myocardial infarction in patients older than 65 years of age to younger patients: the Multicenter Chest Pain Study experience. *Am J Cardiol.* 1989;63:772-776.

69. Rouan GW, Lee TH, Cook EF, Brand DA, Weisberg MC, Goldman L. Clinical characteristics and outcome of acute myocardial infarction in patients with initially normal or nonspecific electrocardiograms (a report from the Multicenter Chest Pain Study). *Am J Cardiol.* 1989;64:1087-1092.

70. Sizemore C, Lewis JF. Clinical relevance of chest pain during dobutamine stress echocardiography in women. *Clin Cardiol.* 1999;22:715-718.

71. Sharaf BL, Pepine CJ, Kerensky RA, Reis SE, Reichek N, Rogers WJ, Sopko G, Kelsey SF, Holubkov R, Olson M, Miele NJ, Williams DO, Merz CN. Detailed angiographic analysis of women with suspected ischemic chest pain (pilot phase data from the NHLBI-sponsored Women's Ischemia Syndrome Evaluation [WISE] Study Angiographic Core Laboratory). *Am J Cardiol*. 2001;87:937-941; A933.

72. Eisenberg MJ, Topol EJ. Prehospital administration of aspirin in patients with unstable angina and acute myocardial infarction. *Arch Intern Med*. 1996;156:1506-1510.

73. Antman EM, Anbe DT, Armstrong PW, Bates ER, Green LA, Hand M, Hochman JS, Krumholz HM, Kushner FG, Lamas GA, Mullany CJ, Ornato JP, Pearle DL, Sloan MA, Smith SC Jr, Alpert JS, Anderson JL, Faxon DP, Fuster V, Gibbons RJ, Gregoratos G, Halperin JL, Hiratzka LF, Hunt SA, Jacobs AK. ACC/AHA guidelines for the management of patients with ST-elevation myocardial infarction: a report of the American College of Cardiology/American Heart Association Task Force on Practice Guidelines (Committee to Revise the 1999 Guidelines for the Management of Patients With Acute Myocardial Infarction). *Circulation*. 2004;110:e82-e292.

74. Pantridge JF, Geddes JS. A mobile intensive-care unit in the management of myocardial infarction. *Lancet*. 1967;2:271-273.

75. Cohen MC, Rohtla KM, Lavery CE, Muller JE, Mittleman MA. Meta-analysis of the morning excess of acute myocardial infarction and sudden cardiac death [published correction appears in *Am J Cardiol*. 1998;81:260]. *Am J Cardiol*. 1997;79:1512-1516.

76. Colquhoun MC, Julien DG. Sudden death in the community—the arrhythmia causing cardiac arrest and results of immediate resuscitation. *Resuscitation*. 1992;24:177A.

77. Campbell RW, Murray A, Julian DG. Ventricular arrhythmias in first 12 hours of acute myocardial infarction: natural history study. *Br Heart J*. 1981;46:351-357.

78. O'Doherty M, Tayler DI, Quinn E, Vincent R, Chamberlain DA. Five hundred patients with myocardial infarction monitored within one hour of symptoms. *Br Med J (Clin Res Ed)*. 1983;286:1405-1408.

79. Lie KI, Wellens HJ, Downar E, Durrer D. Observations on patients with primary ventricular fibrillation complicating acute myocardial infarction. *Circulation*. 1975;52:755-759.

80. The Public Access Defibrillation Trial Investigators. Public-access defibrillation and survival after out-of-hospital cardiac arrest. *N Engl J Med*. 2004;351:637-646.

81. Goodacre S, Locker T, Morris F, Campbell S. How useful are clinical features in the diagnosis of acute, undifferentiated chest pain? *Acad Emerg Med*. 2002;9:203-208.

82. Goodacre SW, Angelini K, Arnold J, Revill S, Morris F. Clinical predictors of acute coronary syndromes in patients with undifferentiated chest pain. *QJM*. 2003;96:893-898.

83. Everts B, Karlson BW, Wahrborg P, Hedner T, Herlitz J. Localization of pain in suspected acute myocardial infarction in relation to final diagnosis, age and sex, and site and type of infarction. *Heart Lung*. 1996;25:430-437.

84. McSweeney JC, Cody M, O'Sullivan P, Elberson K, Moser DK, Garvin BJ. Women's early warning symptoms of acute myocardial infarction. *Circulation*. 2003;108:2619-2623.

85. Canto JG, Rogers WJ, Bowlby LJ, French WJ, Pearce DJ, Weaver WD. The prehospital electrocardiogram in acute myocardial infarction: is its full potential being realized? National Registry of Myocardial Infarction 2 Investigators. *J Am Coll Cardiol*. 1997;29:498-505.

86. Curtis JP, Portnay EL, Wang Y, McNamara RL, Herrin J, Bradley EH, Magid DJ, Blaney ME, Canto JG, Krumholz HM. The pre-hospital electrocardiogram and time to reperfusion in patients with acute myocardial infarction, 2000-2002: findings from the National Registry of Myocardial Infarction-4. *J Am Coll Cardiol*. 2006;47:1544-1552.

87. Weaver W, Cerqueira M, Hallstrom A, Litwin P, Martin J, Kudenchuk P, Eisenberg M. Prehospital-initiated vs hospital-initiated thrombolytic therapy: the Myocardial Infarction Triage and Intervention Trial (MITI). *JAMA*. 1993;270:1203-1210.

88. Foster DB, Dufendach JH, Barkdoll CM, Mitchell BK. Prehospital recognition of AMI using independent nurse/paramedic 12-lead ECG evaluation: impact on in-hospital times to thrombolysis in a rural community hospital. *Am J Emerg Med*. 1994;12:25-31.

89. Millar-Craig MW, Joy AV, Adamowicz M, Furber R, Thomas B. Reduction in treatment delay by paramedic ECG diagnosis of myocardial infarction with direct CCU admission. *Heart*. 1997;78:456-461.

90. Myers RB. Prehospital management of acute myocardial infarction: Electrocardiogram acquisition and interpretation, and thrombolysis by prehospital care providers. *Can J Cardiol*. 1998;14:1231-1240.

91. Ioannidis JP, Salem D, Chew PW, Lau J. Accuracy and clinical effect of out-of-hospital electrocardiography in the diagnosis of acute cardiac ischemia: a meta-analysis. *Ann Emerg Med*. 2001;37:461-470.

92. Morrow DA, Antman EM, Sayah A, Schuhwerk KC, Giugliano RP, deLemos JA, Waller M, Cohen SA, Rosenberg DG, Cutler SS, McCabe CH, Walls RM, Braunwald E. Evaluation of the time saved by prehospital initiation of reteplase for ST-elevation myocardial infarction: results of The Early Retavase-Thrombolysis in Myocardial Infarction (ER-TIMI) 19 trial. *J Am Coll Cardiol*. 2002;40:71-77.

93. Ferguson JD, Brady WJ, Perron AD, Kielar ND, Benner JP, Currance SB, Braithwaite S, Aufderheide TP. The prehospital 12-lead electrocardiogram: Impact on management of the out-of-hospital acute coronary syndrome patient. *Am J Emerg Med*. 2003;21:136-142.

94. Pedley DK, Bissett K, Connolly EM, Goodman CG, Golding I, Pringle TH, McNeill GP, Pringle SD, Jones MC. Prospective observational cohort study of time saved by prehospital thrombolysis for ST elevation myocardial infarction delivered by paramedics. *BMJ*. 2003;327:22-26.

95. Terkelsen CJ, Norgaard BL, Lassen JF, Andersen HR. Prehospital evaluation in ST-elevation myocardial infarction patients treated with primary percutaneous coronary intervention. *J Electrocardiol*. 2005;38:187-192.

96. Terkelsen CJ, Lassen JF, Norgaard BL, Gerdes JC, Poulsen SH, Bendix K, Ankersen JP, Gotzsche LB, Romer FK, Nielsen TT, Andersen HR. Reduction of treatment delay in patients with ST-elevation myocardial infarction: impact of pre-hospital diagnosis and direct referral to primary percutaneous coronary intervention. *Eur Heart J*. 2005;26:770-777.

97. Bjorklund E, Stenestrand U, Lindback J, Svensson L, Wallentin L, Lindahl B. Prehospital diagnosis and start of treatment reduces time delay and mortality in real-life patients with STEMI. *J Electrocardiol*. 2005;38:186.

98. Brainard AH, Raynovich W, Tandberg D, Bedrick EJ. The prehospital 12-lead electrocardiogram's effect on time to initiation of reperfusion therapy: a systematic review and meta-analysis of existing literature. *Am J Emerg Med*. 2005;23:351-356.

99. Hankins DG, Luke A. Emergency medical service aspects of emergency cardiac care. *Emerg Med Clin North Am*. 2005;23:1219-1231.

100. Morrison LJ, Brooks S, Sawadsky B, McDonald A, Verbeek PR. Prehospital 12-lead electrocardiography impact on acute myocardial infarction treatment times and mortality: a systematic review. *Acad Emerg Med*. 2006;13:84-89.

101. Amsterdam EA, Miles P, Turnipseed S, Diercks D. The prehospital ECG: a simple (and effective) tool for a complex problem. *Crit Pathw Cardiol*. 2007;6:64-66.

102. Brown JP, Mahmud E, Dunford JV, Ben-Yehuda O. Effect of prehospital 12-lead electrocardiogram on activation of the cardiac catheterization laboratory and door-to-balloon time in ST-segment elevation acute myocardial infarction. *Am J Cardiol*. 2008;101:158-161.

103. Bradley EH, Herrin J, Wang Y, Barton BA, Webster TR, Mattera JA, Roumanis SA, Curtis JP, Nallamothu BK, Magid DJ, McNamara RL, Parkosewich J, Loeb JM, Krumholz HM. Strategies for reducing the door-to-balloon time in acute myocardial infarction. *N Engl J Med*. 2006;355:2308-2320.

104. Bradley EH, Roumanis SA, Radford MJ, Webster TR, McNamara RL, Mattera JA, Barton BA, Berg DN, Portnay EL, Moscovitz H, Parkosewich J, Holmboe ES, Blaney M, Krumholz HM. Achieving door-to-balloon times that meet quality guidelines: how do successful hospitals do it? *J Am Coll Cardiol*. 2005;46:1236-1241.

105. Bradley EH, Curry LA, Webster TR, Mattera JA, Roumanis SA, Radford MJ, McNamara RL, Barton BA, Berg DN, Krumholz HM. Achieving rapid door-to-balloon times: how top hospitals improve complex clinical systems. *Circulation*. 2006;113:1079-1085.

106. Swor R, Hegerberg S, McHugh-McNally A, Goldstein M, McEachin CC. Prehospital 12-lead ECG: efficacy or effectiveness? *Prehosp Emerg Care*. 2006;10:374-377.

107. Gross BW, Dauterman KW, Moran MG, Kotler TS, Schnugg SJ, Rostykus PS, Ross AM, Weaver WD. An approach to shorten time to infarct artery patency in patients with ST-segment elevation myocardial infarction. *Am J Cardiol*. 2007;99:1360-1363.

108. Dhruva VN, Abdelhadi SI, Anis A, Gluckman W, Hom D, Dougan W, Kaluski E, Haider B, Klapholz M. ST-Segment Analysis Using Wireless Technology in Acute Myocardial Infarction (STAT-MI) trial. *J Am Coll Cardiol*. 2007;50:509-513.

109. Nallamothu BK, Bradley EH, Krumholz HM. Time to treatment in primary percutaneous coronary intervention. *N Engl J Med*. 2007;357:1631-1638.

110. Aufderheide TP, Hendley GE, Thakur RK, Mateer JR, Stueven HA, Olson DW, Hargarten KM, Laitinen F, Robinson N, Preuss KC, et al. The diagnostic impact of prehospital 12-lead electrocardiography. *Ann Emerg Med*. 1990;19:1280-1287.

111. Karagounis L, Ipsen SK, Jessop MR, Gilmore KM, Valenti DA, Clawson JJ, Teichman S, Anderson JL. Impact of field-transmitted electrocardiography on time to in-hospital thrombolytic therapy in acute myocardial infarction. *Am J Cardiol*. 1990;66:786-791.

112. Grim PS, Feldman T, Childers RW. Evaluation of patients for the need of thrombolytic therapy in the prehospital setting. *Ann Emerg Med*. 1989;18:483-488.

113. Kudenchuk PJ, Ho MT, Weaver WD, Litwin PE, Martin JS, Eisenberg MS, Hallstrom AP, Cobb LA, Kennedy JW. Accuracy of computer-interpreted electrocardiography in selecting patients for thrombolytic therapy. MITI Project Investigators. *J Am Coll Cardiol*. 1991;17:1486-1491.

114. Kereiakes DJ, Gibler WB, Martin LH, Pieper KS, Anderson LC. Relative importance of emergency medical system transport and the prehospital electrocardiogram on reducing hospital time delay to therapy for acute myocardial infarction: a preliminary report from the Cincinnati Heart Project. *Am Heart J*. 1992;123:835-840.

115. Aufderheide TP, Kereiakes DJ, Weaver WD, Gibler WB, Simoons ML. Planning, implementation, and process monitoring for prehospital 12-lead ECG diagnostic programs. *Prehosp Disaster Med*. 1996;11:162-171.

116. Williams DM. 2006 JEMS 200-city survey. EMS from all angles. *JEMS*. 2007;32:38-42, 44, 46 passim.

117. Jollis JG, Roettig ML, Aluko AO, Anstrom KJ, Applegate RJ, Babb JD, Berger PB, Bohle DJ, Fletcher SM, Garvey JL, Hathaway WR, Hoekstra JW, Kelly RV, Maddox WT Jr, Shiber JR, Valeri FS, Watling BA, Wilson BH, Granger CB. Implementation of a statewide system for coronary reperfusion for ST-segment elevation myocardial infarction. *JAMA*. 2007;298:2371-2380.

118. Karagounis L, Ipsen SK, Jessop MR, Gilmore KM, Valenti DA, Clawson JJ, Teichman S, Anderson JL. Impact of field-transmitted electrocardiography on time to in-hospital thrombolytic therapy in acute myocardial infarction. *Am J Cardiol*. 1990;66:786-791.

119. Morrison LJ, Visentin LM, Kiss A, Theriault R, Eby D, Vermeulen M, Sherbino J, Verbeek PR. Validation of a rule for termination of resuscitation in out-of-hospital cardiac arrest. *N Engl J Med*. 2006;355:478-487.

120. Grim P, Feldman T, Martin M, Donovan R, Nevins V, Childers RW. Cellular telephone transmission of 12-lead electrocardiograms from ambulance to hospital. *Am J Cardiol*. 1987;60:715-720.

121. Gibler WB, Kereiakes DJ, Dean EN, Martin L, Anderson L, Abbottsmith CW, Blanton J, Blanton D, Morris JA Jr, Gibler CD, et al. Prehospital diagnosis and treatment of acute myocardial infarction: a north-south perspective: the Cincinnati Heart Project and the Nashville Prehospital TPA Trial. *Am Heart J*. 1991;121(pt 1):1-11.

122. Aufderheide TP, Keelan MH, Hendley GE, Robinson NA, Hastings TE, Lewin RF, Hewes HF, Daniel A, Engle D, Gimbel BK, et al. Milwaukee Prehospital Chest Pain Project—phase I: feasibility and accuracy of prehospital thrombolytic candidate selection. *Am J Cardiol*. 1992;69:991-996.

123. Weaver WD. Time to thrombolytic treatment: factors affecting delay and their influence on outcome. *J Am Coll Cardiol*. 1995;25(suppl):3S-9S.

124. Kudenchuk PJ, Maynard C, Cobb LA, Wirkus M, Martin JS, Kennedy JW, Weaver WD. Utility of the prehospital electrocardiogram in diagnosing acute coronary syndromes: the Myocardial Infarction Triage and Intervention (MITI) Project. *J Am Coll Cardiol*. 1998;32:17-27.

125. Massel D, Dawdy JA, Melendez LJ. Strict reliance on a computer algorithm or measurable ST segment criteria may lead to errors in thrombolytic therapy eligibility. *Am Heart J*. 2000;140:221-226.

126. Terkelsen CJ, Norgaard BL, Lassen JF, Gerdes JC, Ankersen JP, Romer F, Nielsen TT, Andersen HR. Telemedicine used for remote prehospital diagnosing in patients suspected of acute myocardial infarction. *J Intern Med*. 2002;252:412-420.

127. Campbell PT, Patterson J, Cromer D, Wall K, Adams GL, Albano A, Corey C, Fox P, Gardner J, Hawthorne B, Lipton J, Sejersten M, Thompson A, Wilfong S, Maynard C, Wagner G. Prehospital triage of acute myocardial infarction: wireless transmission of electrocardiograms to the on-call cardiologist via a handheld computer. *J Electrocardiol*. 2005;38:300-309.

128. Clemmensen P, Sejersten M, Sillesen M, Hampton D, Wagner GS, Loumann-Nielsen S. Diversion of ST-elevation myocardial infarction patients for primary angioplasty based on wireless prehospital 12-lead electrocardiographic transmission directly to the cardiologist's handheld computer: a progress report. *J Electrocardiol*. 2005;38:194-198.

129. Young D, Barbagelata A, Wagner G. Have we made progress in reducing time to reperfusion in the management of acute myocardial infarction? A last decade overview. The potential key role of wireless electrocardiographic transmission. *J Electrocardiol*. 2005;38:94-95.

130. Adams GL, Campbell PT, Adams JM, Strauss DG, Wall K, Patterson J, Shuping KB, Maynard C, Young D, Corey C, Thompson A, Lee BA, Wagner GS. Effectiveness of prehospital wireless transmission of electrocardiograms to a cardiologist via hand-held device for patients with acute myocardial infarction (from the Timely Intervention in Myocardial Emergency, NorthEast Experience [TIME-NE]). *Am J Cardiol*. 2006;98:1160-1164.

131. Vaught C, Young DR, Bell SJ, Maynard C, Gentry M, Jacubowitz S, Leibrandt PN, Munsey D, Savona MR, Wall TC, Wagner GS. The failure of years of experience with electrocardiographic transmission from paramedics to the hospital emergency department to reduce the delay from door to primary coronary intervention below the 90-minute threshold during acute myocardial infarction. *J Electrocardiol*. 2006;39:136-141.

132. Davis DP, Graydon C, Stein R, Wilson S, Buesch B, Berthiaume S, Lee DM, Rivas J, Vilke GM, Leahy DR. The positive predictive value of paramedic versus emergency physician interpretation of the prehospital 12-lead electrocardiogram. *Prehosp Emerg Care*. 2007;11:399-402.

133. Strauss DG, Sprague PQ, Underhill K, Maynard C, Adams GL, Kessenich A, Sketch MH Jr, Berger PB, Marcozzi D, Granger CB, Wagner GS. Paramedic transtelephonic communication to cardiologist of clinical and electrocardiographic assessment for rapid reperfusion of ST-elevation myocardial infarction. *J Electrocardiol*. 2007;40:265-270.

134. Wall T, Albright J, Livingston B, Isley L, Young D, Nanny M, Jacobowitz S, Maynard C, Mayer N, Pierce K, Rathbone C, Stuckey T, Savona M, Leibrandt P, Brodie B, Wagner G. Prehospital ECG transmission speeds reperfusion for patients with acute myocardial infarction. *N C Med J*. 2000;61:104-108.

135. Brinfield K. Identification of ST elevation AMI on prehospital 12 lead ECG: accuracy of unaided paramedic interpretation. *J Emerg Med*. 1998;16:22S.

136. Hill R, Heller M, Rosenau A, Melanson S, Pronchik D, Patterson J, Gulick H. Paramedic interpretation of prehospital lead-II ST-segments. *Prehosp Disaster Med*. 1997;12:141-144.

137. Sejersten M, Pahlm O, Pettersson J, Zhou S, Maynard C, Feldman CL, Wagner GS. Comparison of EASI-derived 12-lead electrocardiograms versus paramedic-acquired 12-lead electrocardiograms using Mason-Likar limb lead configuration in patients with chest pain. *J Electrocardiol*. 2006; 39:13-21.

138. Feldman JA, Brinsfield K, Bernard S, White D, Maciejko T. Real-time paramedic compared with blinded physician identification of ST-segment elevation myocardial infarction: results of an observational study. *Am J Emerg Med*. 2005; 23:443-448.

139. Whitbread M, Leah V, Bell T, Coats TJ. Recognition of ST elevation by paramedics. *Emerg Med J*. 2002;19:66-67.

140. Giovas P, Papadoyannis D, Thomakos D, Papazachos G, Rallidis M, Soulis D, Stamatopoulos C, Mavrogeni S, Katsilambros N. Transmission of electrocardiograms from a moving ambulance. *J Telemed Telecare*. 1998;4:5-7.

141. Papouchado M, Cox H, Bailey J, White W, Spreadbury T. Early experience with transmission of data from moving ambulances to improve the care of patients with myocardial infarction. *J Telemed Telecare*. 2001;7:27-28.

142. Scholz KH, Hilgers R, Ahlersmann D, Duwald H, Nitsche R, von Knobelsdorff G, Volger B, Moller K, Keating FK. Contact-to-balloon time and door-to-balloon time after initiation of a formalized data feedback in patients with acute ST-elevation myocardial infarction. *Am J Cardiol*. 2008;101:46-52.

143. Rawles JM, Kenmure AC. Controlled trial of oxygen in uncomplicated myocardial infarction. *Br Med J*. 1976;1:1121-1123.

144. Maroko PR, Radvany P, Braunwald E, Hale SL. Reduction of infarct size by oxygen inhalation following acute coronary occlusion. *Circulation*. 1975;52:360-368.

145. Madias JE, Madias NE, Hood WB Jr. Precordial ST-segment mapping. 2. Effects of oxygen inhalation on ischemic injury in patients with acute myocardial infarction. *Circulation*. 1976;53:411-417.

146. O'Neill WW, Martin JL, Dixon SR, Bartorelli AL, Trabattoni D, Oemrawsingh PV, Atsma DE, Chang M, Marquardt W, Oh JK, Krucoff MW, Gibbons RJ, Spears JR. Acute Myocardial Infarction with Hyperoxemic Therapy (AMIHOT): a prospective, randomized trial of intracoronary hyperoxemic reperfusion after percutaneous coronary intervention. *J Am Coll Cardiol*. 2007;50:397-405.

147. Ribeiro LG, Louie EK, Davis MA, Maroko PR. Augmentation of collateral blood flow to the ischaemic myocardium by oxygen inhalation following experimental coronary artery occlusion. *Cardiovasc Res*. 1979;13:160-166.

148. Kelly RF, Hursey TL, Parrillo JE, Schaer GL. Effect of 100% oxygen administration on infarct size and left ventricular function in a canine model of myocardial infarction and reperfusion. *Am Heart J*. 1995;130:957-965.

149. Ishikawa K, Kanamasa K, Yamakado T, Katori R. The beneficial effects of 40% and 100% O2 inhalations on acutely-induced myocardial ischemia in dogs. *Tohoku J Exp Med*. 1986;149:107-117.

150. Madias JE, Hood WB Jr. Reduction of precordial ST-segment elevation in patients with anterior myocardial infarction by oxygen breathing. *Circulation*. 1976;53(suppl):I198-I200.

151. Wilson AT, Channer KS. Hypoxaemia and supplemental oxygen therapy in the first 24 hours after myocardial infarction: the role of pulse oximetry. *J R Coll Physicians Lond*. 1997;31:657-661.

152. Randomised trial of intravenous streptokinase, oral aspirin, both, or neither among 17,187 cases of suspected acute myocardial infarction: ISIS-2. ISIS-2 (Second International Study of Infarct Survival) Collaborative Group. *Lancet*. 1988;2:349-360.

153. Collaborative overview of randomised trials of antiplatelet therapy—I: prevention of death, myocardial infarction, and stroke by prolonged antiplatelet therapy in various categories of patients. Antiplatelet Trialists' Collaboration. *BMJ*. 1994;308:81-106.

154. ISIS-4: a randomised factorial trial assessing early oral captopril, oral mononitrate, and intravenous magnesium sulphate in 58,050 patients with suspected acute myocardial infarction. ISIS-4 (Fourth International Study of Infarct Survival) Collaborative Group. *Lancet*. 1995;345:669-685.

155. European Myocardial Infarction Project Group (EMIP). Prehospital thrombolytic therapy in patients with suspected acute myocardial infarction. The European Myocardial Infarction Project Group. *N Engl J Med*. 1993;329:383-389.

156. Morrison LJ, Verbeek PR, McDonald AC, Sawadsky BV, Cook DJ. Mortality and prehospital thrombolysis for acute myocardial infarction: a meta-analysis. *JAMA*. 2000;283:2686-2692.

157. Weaver WD, Cerqueira M, Hallstrom AP, Litwin PE, Martin JS, Kudenchuk PJ, Eisenberg M. Prehospital-initiated vs hospital-initiated thrombolytic therapy. The Myocardial Infarction Triage and Intervention Trial. *JAMA*. 1993;270:1211-1216.

158. Wallentin L, Goldstein P, Armstrong PW, Granger CB, Adgey AA, Arntz HR, Bogaerts K, Danays T, Lindahl B, Makijarvi M, Verheugt F, Van de Werf F. Efficacy and safety of tenecteplase in combination with the low-molecular-weight heparin enoxaparin or unfractionated heparin in the prehospital setting: the Assessment of the Safety and Efficacy of a New Thrombolytic Regimen (ASSENT)-3 PLUS randomized trial in acute myocardial infarction. *Circulation*. 2003;108:135-142.

159. Morrow DA, Antman EM, Sayah A, Schuhwerk KC, Giugliano RP, deLemos JA, Waller M, Cohen SA, Rosenberg DG, Cutler SS, McCabe CH, Walls RM, Braunwald E. Evaluation of the time saved by prehospital initiation of reteplase for ST-elevation myocardial infarction: results of the Early Retavase–Thrombolysis in Myocardial Infarction (ER-TIMI) 19 trial. *J Am Coll Cardiol*. 2002;40:71-77.

160. Kontos MC, McQueen RH, Jesse RL, Tatum JL, Ornato JP. Can myocardial infarction be rapidly identified in emergency department patients who have left bundle-branch block? *Ann Emerg Med*. 2001;37:431-438.

161. Fesmire FM, Percy RF, Wears RL, MacMath TL. Initial ECG in Q wave and non-Q wave myocardial infarction. *Ann Emerg Med*. 1989;18:741-746.

162. Gallagher EJ. Which patients with suspected myocardial ischemia and left bundle-branch block should receive thrombolytic agents? *Ann Emerg Med*. 2001;37:439-444.

163. Sgarbossa EB, Pinski SL, Wagner GS. Left bundle-branch block and the ECG in diagnosis of acute myocardial infarction. *JAMA*. 1999;282:1224-1225.

164. Sgarbossa EB. Recent advances in the electrocardiographic diagnosis of myocardial infarction: left bundle branch block and pacing. *Pacing Clin Electrophysiol*. 1996;19:1370-1379.

165. Sgarbossa EB. Value of the ECG in suspected acute myocardial infarction with left bundle branch block. *J Electrocardiol*. 2000;33(suppl):87-92.

166. Ryan TJ, Anderson JL, Antman EM, Braniff BA, Brooks NH, Califf RM, Hillis LD, Hiratzka LF, Rapaport E, Riegel BJ, Russell RO, Smith EE III, Weaver WD. ACC/AHA guidelines for the management of patients with acute myocardial infarction: executive summary. A report of the American College of Cardiology/American Heart Association Task Force on Practice Guidelines (Committee on Management of Acute Myocardial Infarction). *Circulation*. 1996;94:2341-2350.

167. Go AS, Barron HV, Rundle AC, Ornato JP, Avins AL. Bundle-branch block and in-hospital mortality in acute myocardial infarction. National Registry of Myocardial Infarction 2 Investigators. *Ann Intern Med*. 1998;129:690-697.

168. Dubois C, Pierard LA, Smeets JP, Foidart G, Legrand V, Kulbertus HE. Short- and long-term prognostic importance of complete bundle-branch block complicating acute myocardial infarction. *Clin Cardiol*. 1988;11:292-296.

169. Ricou F, Nicod P, Gilpin E, Henning H, Ross J Jr. Influence of right bundle branch block on short- and long-term survival after inferior wall Q-wave myocardial infarction. *Am J Cardiol*. 1991;67:1143-1146.

170. Newby KH, Pisano E, Krucoff MW, Green C, Natale A. Incidence and clinical relevance of the occurrence of bundle-branch block in patients treated with thrombolytic therapy. *Circulation*. 1996;94:2424-2428.

171. Moreno AM, Alberola AG, Tomas JG, Chavarri MV, Soria FC, Sanchez EM, Sanchez JG. Incidence and prognostic significance of right bundle branch block in patients with acute myocardial infarction receiving thrombolytic therapy. *Int J Cardiol*. 1997;61:135-141.

172. Melgarejo-Moreno A, Galcera-Tomas J, Garcia-Alberola A, Valdes-Chavarri M, Castillo-Soria FJ, Mira-Sanchez E, Gil-Sanchez J, Allegue-Gallego J. Incidence, clinical characteristics, and prognostic significance of right bundle-branch block in acute myocardial infarction: a study in the thrombolytic era. *Circulation*. 1997;96:1139-1144.

173. Sgarbossa EB, Pinski SL, Topol EJ, Califf RM, Barbagelata A, Goodman SG, Gates KB, Granger CB, Miller DP, Underwood DA, Wagner GS. Acute myocardial infarction and complete bundle branch block at hospital admission: clinical characteristics and outcome in the thrombolytic era. GUSTO-I Investigators. Global Utilization of Streptokinase and t-PA [tissue-type plasminogen activator] for Occluded Coronary Arteries. *J Am Coll Cardiol*. 1998;31:105-110.

174. Gunnarsson G, Eriksson P, Dellborg M. Bundle branch block and acute myocardial infarction. Treatment and outcome. *Scand Cardiovasc J*. 2000;34:575-579.

175. Brilakis ES, Wright RS, Kopecky SL, Reeder GS, Williams BA, Miller WL. Bundle branch block as a predictor of long-term survival after acute myocardial infarction. *Am J Cardiol*. 2001;88:205-209.

176. Alpert JS, Thygesen K, Antman E, Bassand JP. Myocardial infarction redefined—a consensus document of The Joint European Society of Cardiology/American College of Cardiology Committee for the Redefinition of Myocardial Infarction. *J Am Coll Cardiol*. 2000;36:959-969.

177. Wu AH, Apple FS, Gibler WB, Jesse RL, Warshaw MM, Valdes R. National Academy of Clinical Biochemistry Standards of Laboratory Practice: recommendations for the use of cardiac markers in coronary artery diseases. *Clin Chem*. 1999;45:1104-1121.

178. Hjalmarson A, Herlitz J, Holmberg S, Ryden L, Swedberg K, Vedin A, Waagstein F, Waldenstrom A, Waldenstrom J, Wedel H, Wilhelmsen L, Wilhelmsson C. The Göteborg metoprolol trial. Effects on mortality and morbidity in acute myocardial infarction. *Circulation*. 1983;67(6 pt 2):I26-I32.

179. Hjalmarson A, Herlitz J. Limitation of infarct size by beta blockers and its potential role for prognosis. *Circulation*. 1983;67(6 pt 2):I68-I71.

180. The MIAMI Trial Research Group. Metoprolol in acute myocardial infarction (MIAMI): a randomised placebo-controlled international trial. *Eur Heart J*. 1985;6:199-226.

181. Sleight P, Yusuf S, Peto R, Rossi P, Ramsdale D, Bennett D, Bray C, Furse L. Early intravenous atenolol treatment in suspected acute myocardial infarction. *Acta Med Scand Suppl*. 1981;210:185-192.

182. Randomised trial of intravenous atenolol among 16 027 cases of suspected acute myocardial infarction: ISIS-1. First International Study of Infarct Survival Collaborative Group. *Lancet*. 1986;2:57-66.

183. Rehnqvist N, Olsson G, Erhardt L, Ekman AM. Metoprolol in acute myocardial infarction reduces ventricular arrhythmias both in the early stage and after the acute event. *Int J Cardiol*. 1987;15:301-308.

184. Roberts R, Rogers WJ, Mueller HS, Lambrew CT, Diver DJ, Smith HC, Willerson JT, Knatterud GL, Forman S, Passamani E, et al. Immediate versus deferred beta-blockade following thrombolytic therapy in patients with acute myocardial infarction. Results of the Thrombolysis in Myocardial Infarction (TIMI) II-B study. *Circulation*. 1991;83:422-437.

185. Chen ZM, Pan HC, Chen YP, Peto R, Collins R, Jiang LX, Xie JX, Liu LS. Early intravenous then oral metoprolol in 45 852 patients with acute myocardial infarction: randomised placebo-controlled trial. *Lancet*. 2005;366:1622-1632.

186. Wallentin L, Bergstrand L, Dellborg M, Fellenius C, Granger CB, Lindahl B, Lins LE, Nilsson T, Pehrsson K, Siegbahn A, Swahn E. Low molecular weight heparin (dalteparin) compared to unfractionated heparin as an adjunct to rt-PA (alteplase) for improvement of coronary artery patency in acute myocardial infarction—the ASSENT Plus study. *Eur Heart J*. 2003;24:897-908.

187. Ross AM, Molhoek P, Lundergan C, Knudtson M, Draoui Y, Regalado L, Le Louer V, Bigonzi F, Schwartz W, De Jong E, Coyne K. Randomized comparison of enoxaparin, a low-molecular-weight heparin, with unfractionated heparin adjunctive to recombinant tissue plasminogen activator thrombolysis and aspirin: Second Trial of Heparin and Aspirin Reperfusion Therapy (HART II). *Circulation*. 2001;104:648-652.

188. Van de Werf FJ, Armstrong PW, Granger C, Wallentin L. Efficacy and safety of tenecteplase in combination with enoxaparin, abciximab, or unfractionated heparin: the ASSENT-3 randomised trial in acute myocardial infarction. *Lancet*. 2001;358:605-613.

189. Theroux P, Welsh RC. Meta-analysis of randomized trials comparing enoxaparin versus unfractionated heparin as adjunctive therapy to fibrinolysis in ST-elevation acute myocardial infarction. *Am J Cardiol*. 2003;91:860-864.

190. Baird SH, Menown IB, McBride SJ, Trouton TG, Wilson C. Randomized comparison of enoxaparin with unfractionated heparin following fibrinolytic therapy for acute myocardial infarction. *Eur Heart J*. 2002;23:627-632.

191. Sabatine MS, Cannon CP, Gibson CM, Lopez-Sendon JL, Montalescot G, Theroux P, Claeys MJ, Cools F, Hill KA, Skene AM, McCabe CH, Braunwald E. Addition of clopidogrel to aspirin and fibrinolytic therapy for myocardial infarction with ST-segment elevation. *N Engl J Med*. 2005;352:1179-1189.

192. Chen ZM, Jiang LX, Chen YP, Xie JX, Pan HC, Peto R, Collins R, Liu LS. Addition of clopidogrel to aspirin in 45 852 patients with acute myocardial infarction: randomised placebo-controlled trial. *Lancet*. 2005;366:1607-1621.

193. Wiviott SD, Antman EM, Gibson CM, Montalescot G, Riesmeyer J, Weerakkody G, Winters KJ, Warmke JW, McCabe CH, Braunwald E; TRITON-TIMI 38 Investigators. Evaluation of prasugrel compared with clopidogrel in patients with acute coronary syndromes: design and rationale for the TRial to assess Improvement in Therapeutic Outcomes by optimizing platelet InhibitioN with prasugrel Thrombolysis In Myocardial Infarction 38 (TRITON-TIMI 38). *Am Heart J*. 2006;152:627-635.

194. Wiviott SD, Braunwald E, McCabe CH, Montalescot G, Ruzyllo W, Gottlieb S, Neumann FJ, Ardissino D, De Servi S, Murphy SA, Riesmeyer J, Weerakkody G, Gibson CM, Antman EM; TRITON-TIMI 38 Investigators. Prasugrel versus clopidogrel in patients with acute coronary syndromes. *N Engl J Med*. 2007;357:2001-2015.

195. Grines CL, Bonow RO, Casey DE Jr, Gardner TJ, Lockhart PB, Moliterno DJ, O'Gara P, Whitlow P; American Heart Association; American College of Cardiology; Society for Cardiovascular Angiography and Interventions; American College of Surgeons; American Dental Association; American College of Physicians. Prevention of premature discontinuation of dual antiplatelet therapy in patients with coronary artery stents: a science advisory from the American Heart Association, American College of Cardiology, Society for Cardiovascular Angiography and Interventions, American College of Surgeons, and American Dental Association, with representation from the American College of Physicians. *J Am Dent Assoc*. 2007;138:652-655.

196. Hochholzer W, Trenk D, Frundi D, Blanke P, Fischer B, Andris K, Bestehorn HP, Büttner HJ, Neumann FJ. Time dependence of platelet inhibition after a 600-mg loading dose of clopidogrel in a large, unselected cohort of candidates for percutaneous coronary intervention. *Circulation*. 2005;111:2560-2564.

197. Smith SC Jr, Feldman TE, Hirshfeld JW Jr, Jacobs AK, Kern MJ, King SB III, Morrison DA, O'Neill WW, Schaff HV, Whitlow PL, Williams DO, Antman EM, Smith SC Jr, Adams CD, Anderson JL, Faxon DP, Fuster V, Halperin JL, Hiratzka LF, Hunt SA, Jacobs AK, Nishimura R, Ornato JP, Page RL, Riegel B; American College of Cardiology/American Heart Association Task Force on Practice Guidelines; ACC/AHA/SCAI Writing Committee to Update the 2001 Guidelines for Percutaneous Coronary Intervention. ACC/AHA/SCAI 2005 guideline update for percutaneous coronary intervention: a report of the American College of Cardiology/American Heart Association Task Force on Practice Guidelines (ACC/AHA/SCAI Writing Committee to Update the 2001 Guidelines for Percutaneous Coronary Intervention). *J Am Coll Cardiol*. 2006;47:e1-e121.

198. Plavix (clopidogrel bisulfate) [package insert]. Bridgewater, NJ: Bristol-Myers Squibb Sanofi-aventis; 2009.

199. Kim JH, Newby LK, Clare RM, Shaw LK, Lodge AJ, Smith PK, Jolicoeur EM, Rao SV, Becker RC, Mark DB, Granger CB. Clopidogrel use and bleeding after coronary artery bypass graft surgery. *Am Heart J*. 2008;156:886-892.

200. Bonello L, Camoin-Jau L, Arques S, Boyer C, Panagides D, Wittenberg O, Simeoni MC, Barragan P, Dignat-George F, Paganelli F. Adjusted clopidogrel loading doses according to vasodilator-stimulated phosphoprotein phosphorylation index decrease rate of major adverse cardiovascular events in patients with clopidogrel resistance: a multicenter randomized prospective study. *J Am Coll Cardiol*. 2008;51:1404-1411.

201. Correia LC, Sposito AC, Lima JC, Magalhaes LP, Passos LC, Rocha MS, D'Oliveira A, Esteves JP. Anti-inflammatory effect of atorvastatin (80 mg) in unstable angina pectoris and non-Q-wave acute myocardial infarction. *Am J Cardiol*. 2003;92:298-301.

202. Kayikcioglu M, Can L, Evrengul H, Payzin S, Kultursay H. The effect of statin therapy on ventricular late potentials in acute myocardial infarction. *Int J Cardiol*. 2003;90:63-72.

203. Kayikcioglu M, Can L, Kultursay H, Payzin S, Turkoglu C. Early use of pravastatin in patients with acute myocardial infarction undergoing coronary angioplasty. *Acta Cardiol*. 2002;57:295-302.

204. Kinlay S, Schwartz GG, Olsson AG, Rifai N, Leslie SJ, Sasiela WJ, Szarek M, Libby P, Ganz P. High-dose atorvastatin enhances the decline in inflammatory markers in patients with acute coronary syndromes in the MIRACL study. *Circulation*. 2003;108:1560-1566.

205. MacMahon S, Collins R, Peto R, Koster RW, Yusuf S. Effects of prophylactic lidocaine in suspected acute myocardial infarction. An overview of results from the randomized, controlled trials. *JAMA*. 1988;260:1910-1916.

206. Savonitto S, Ardissino D, Granger CB, Morando G, Prando MD, Mafrici A, Cavallini C, Melandri G, Thompson TD, Vahanian A, Ohman EM, Califf RM, Van de Werf F, Topol EJ. Prognostic value of the admission electrocardiogram in acute coronary syndromes. *JAMA*. 1999;281:707-713.

207. Spodick DH. Differential characteristics of the electrocardiogram in early repolarization and acute pericarditis. *N Engl J Med*. 1976;295:523-526.

208. Wang K, Asinger RW, Marriott HJ. ST-segment elevation in conditions other than acute myocardial infarction. *N Engl J Med*. 2003;349:2128-2135.